Dedication

This book is dedicated to my dearly loved mom, Gloria Ann Stevenson. She was one of the most creative people I've ever known.

Acknowledgements

I thank God, first and foremost, and am also especially thankful for these very dear people:

Kait and Alina, who were my supercell of brainstormers and project testers. Sam, who said it was okay if I put off finishing his quilt and let me know he was proud of me. Gonzo, who always got that business light in his eyes when he saw my work.

Jim and Cindy, who were my diligent in-house editors. Kathy, whose enthusiastic reactions were like having my own booster club.

For Lynn, who told me I should write this book, gave me pep talks when my courage failed, and cheered me on every step of the way.

For Julie who asked, "Do you have any bindings you would like me to sew?" and embroidered beautiful labels for me, even when her own schedule was packed to the rafters.

To both Julie and Valerie who kicked my work up to a whole higher level with their beautiful quilting.

For my friends in Quilting Blogland, who gave me unwavering encouragement and support.

And last, but not least, I would like to express my heartfelt thanks to Ginny Harris, Adriana Fitch, Sarah Bozone, Chris Gilbert, Caitlin Ridings, Elaine Wilson, Charles Lynch, and the rest of the editorial and design staff at the AQS. A special thank you goes to Elaine Brelsford for giving me this wonderful opportunity and to Kimberly Tetrev for working to make my dream a reality. It could not have happened without you all!

Crafted Appliqué: New Possibilities · · · · Lara Buccella

Contents

Introduction 6
    What is Crafted Appliqué? 7
    Seeing Is Believing 8

The Process 10
    Comparing the Different Formulas .. 10
    Tools and Supplies 12
    Working with the Patterns........ 12
    Fabric Preparation 13
    Laying out and Applying Appliqués . 18
    Stitching the Appliqués 19

The Projects 23
    CHUBBY CHECKERS 24
    FOLK ART CHRISTMAS.......... 29
    THE WALKING TREE 33
    CECROPIA UTOPIA............. 39
    IT'S SUPER QUILTER! 45
    HELLO MR. RANGER, SIR! 55
    CATMINT COTTAGE 66

Patterns 82
Resources 95
About the Author 95

Lara Buccella ····· **Crafted Appliqué:** New Possibilities

Introduction

It is true that many quilters hesitate or even run the other way when it comes to doing appliqué. You would laugh if you knew all the reactions from people when they learned that I was writing a book on appliqué quilting. One of the funniest was my friend Sandra. Even though she is quite good at appliqué, she jokingly refers to it as "Aaaack-pliqué" and she hopes that this book will "change that to *Ahhh-pliqué*, said with a sigh of contentment."

That's how I initially felt about appliqué too. My hand stitching has never been a thing of beauty. I was afraid to try appliqué quilting because of this. I then learned about machine stitched, raw edge appliqué and gave it a go, with mixed results.

Until recently, my two favorite methods for adhering appliqués to the fabric before stitching were to either use a glue stick or iron-on fusible web. These are good methods and they both have specific uses that work well.

They also have their difficulties with fraying, which is fine if that is the look you are going for, or you don't mind a few messy edges. To minimize fraying, it is important to be accurate when you sew; you don't have a large margin of error. When you stitch too far from the edge, your appliqué won't hold up well. If you stitch too close to the edge, you end up with a frayed edge and a detached appliqué, right off the bat. All this accuracy takes practice and close attention. Also, these two methods often do not hold up well with frequent handling and sometimes fray when it comes time to quilt over them.

What can you do if you want to machine stitch your appliqués, but want the edge of the appliqué to still look great after all your work is done? How about a technique that will keep looking neat and tidy, even after regular handling or laundering?

Crafted Appliqué is a new way to do raw edge appliqué. Think of it as "Not So Raw Edge" appliqué. Even if you already know how to appliqué to your heart's content, you will find that this method opens up new possibilities. It's a great technique to have in your bag of tricks. I hope you will like making some of the original projects in this book and that they will provide a springboard for your own creativity.

Introduction

What is Crafted Appliqué?

Are you someone who likes to experiment? I am. For instance, I have a habit of not following recipes exactly. When I get in a creative mood, I like to play around with things and see what happens. I find this to be the most fun! So, one day while messing around with sewing ideas (and I do mean "messing"), I discovered something that makes raw edge appliqué a much more forgiving form of quilting.

This time I was playing with Mod Podge® and the results were very exciting. You may be familiar with Mod Podge. It's a terrific product that has been around for decades. You may have first used it for decoupage. Nowadays, Plaid® makes many formulas to serve a wide variety of purposes. Mod Podge can be used to work with fabric and Plaid makes a formula specifically with this in mind.

Crafted Appliqué is unlike any other method of preparing appliqués because it uses Mod Podge in an unexpected and completely new way: as an iron-on treatment for your appliqué pieces. To understand how useful this new technique is, let's compare it with two other methods used for machine sewn, raw edge appliqué: Fusible web and Glue sticks.

METHOD COMPARISON CHART			
	Fusible Web	Glue Sticks	Crafted Appliqué
Sticking Factor	Once ironed on, cannot be moved without damaging the applique.	Can fall off quickly	Adheres well, and can be repositioned and re-ironed many times.
Fraying	Have to carefully sew along the edges as they can peel up and fray a little from wear and tear.	Have to be very careful while handling and sewing as they fray easily.	Holds up well to rough treatment, various sewing techniques, washing, and ironing.
Expense	Most Expensive	Cheapest	Middle of the road cost
Prep time	Still a timely investment.	Least amount of time, unless you count repeated handwashing.	Takes the longest, but it saves you time in the end and is less frustrating.
Cleanliness	If you mess up and have to move a piece, it leaves hard to remove residue on the background fabric.	Can make fingers a sticky mess, which leads to further fraying.	Pre-treatment allows for a clean workspace, hands, and tools.
Laundering	Can be laundered, but it wears on the fabric and appliqués.	Should not be laundered, unless you desire the frayed look.	Can be laundered and still looks good.

Introduction

Other Benefits to Crafted Appliqué Include:

You can iron paper patterns onto the back side of treated fabric and then cut them out, peel off the pattern and then press the appliqué to your background fabric. The appliqué will adhere perfectly, yet is easily repositioned.

If you use Mod Podge for Fabric, you can finger press smaller pattern pieces on the back of the treated fabric. This allows you to move the cutouts closer together, saving on fabric.

You don't have to worry about your pieces stretching or distorting along the bias grain of the fabric.

You can make light colored fabrics less transparent, with a process I call back-coating.

It allows you to appliqué finely cut, detailed shapes that would otherwise break apart and be quite difficult to sew using other raw edge methods.

It keeps looking good longer on items that receive frequent handling. Because of this, appliqués can boldly go where no appliqué has gone before.

Seeing is Believing

This chapter is a demonstration comparing three different methods for adhering appliqués when doing machine stitched, raw edge appliqué:

1. Using a glue stick

2. Using fusible web interfacing

3. Using the Crafted Appliqué method with Fabric Mod Podge

To make the comparison fair, I used die cut oak leaves for each example. An oak leaf is a pretty tricky shape. With all those curves, fraying is inevitable. This is a quilter's version of a controlled experiment.

After sewing the appliqués on, I put the test samples all in our washing machine in the same load, set it on delicate and washed in warm water. Next, I put them in the dryer to tumble dry on medium heat. After I took them out of the dryer, I did nothing to make them look better, such as ironing them.

You can see the results in the following examples.

The Rust colored leaves, prepared with Mod Podge (fig. 3) have almost zero fraying. They look practically the same as they looked before they were washed. The world of possibilities that this opens up is very exciting. Just think what you could do with appliqués that fray so little!

Introduction

I am embarrassed for the Navy glue stick appliqués. They looked like they were having a bad day even before they were washed (fig. 1).

The Jade Green fusible web appliqués look a bit worn and frazzled. If I had used a zigzag or blanket stitch they probably would have held up better (fig. 2).

Clearly, Crafted Appliqué is the best method for work where you want appliqués to hold up well and stay looking neat, with no fraying (fig. 3). It has about the same stiffness as fusible web interfacing. It provides a much sturdier edge for all machine appliqué stitches. This allows for you to machine stitch appliques with greater detail. Even if you never intend to wash an item, appliqués sewn with this method will still hold up better over the years.

The ability to sew down appliqués without always having to stitch along the edges opens up a whole new world of possibilities. When sewn only in the veins of the leaf, as shown in the example on the right side of each photo, Crafted Appliqué held up very well and even lent a little three dimensional effect after washing and drying. Stitching along the veins of the leaves is not only easier and more fun, but it is quite pretty too!

With this method, you can now choose appliqué patterns and projects that would have been impractical before. You will be able to look at an appliqué and ask yourself where you want to stitch, instead of the appliqué completely dictating where you have to stitch.

Fig. 1. Navy appliqués using the glue stick method.

Fig. 2. Jade Green appliqués using fusible web interfacing.

Fig. 3. Rust appliqués using the Crafted Appliqué method.

The Process

Comparing the Different Formulas

In my "controlled" experiments, I tested three of the many Mod Podge formulas in order to learn how well each one works for iron-on appliqué (figs. 1 and 2).

As you might guess, for the purposes of appliqué, the properties of each formula lend itself to various uses.

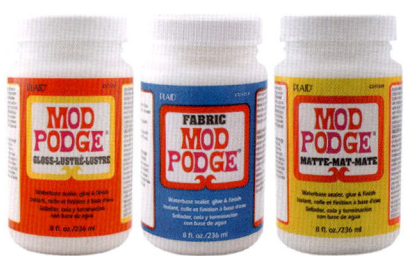

Fig. 1. Three Mod Podge formulas

THREE DIFFERENT MOD PODGE FORMULAS AND THEIR APPLICATIONS FOR APPLIQUÉ			
Properties	Fabric Mod Podge	Mod Podge Matte	Mod Podge Gloss
Ability of treated fabric to form a strong bond when ironed onto another fabric	Adheres very well and won't let go with normal handling. Appliqués peel off easily and can be repositioned many times.	Adheres very well and won't let go with normal handling. Appliqués peel off easily and can be repositioned many times.	This formula has the strongest bond of all. Appliqués are very difficult to peel off and doing so might damage the appliqué.
Ability to finger press or iron paper patterns to the treated side of fabric and then easily remove them	Paper patterns can be ironed on and easily peeled off. This is the formula to use if you wish to finger press small pattern pieces to the back of treated fabric.	Patterns can be ironed onto the back of treated fabric and then easily removed.	Care must be taken to use the lowest setting on your iron, otherwise it is difficult to remove paper patterns unless you dampen them.
Ability of treated fabrics to keep their shape and clean edge after laundering	Mod Podge for Fabric holds up incredibly well when laundered.	Washing is not recommended. If need be, items can be sponged clean.	Washing is not recommended. If need be, items can be sponged clean.
Flexibility and drape of treated fabrics	Fabric treated with this formula is a little thicker, but stays supple and drapes well.	Fabric treated with this formula is a little stiffer. Appliqués become slightly less flexible.	Fabric treated with this formula is slightly stiff. This makes it perfect for projects that need a more rigid surface.

Fig. 2. Mod Podge chart

The Fabric Mod Podge formula is the only one to use when the item will be laundered regularly. Also, for thinner and lighter weight fabrics, the Fabric formula works best. It is thicker than the other formulas and is less likely to soak through to the front of thin fabrics. The Fabric formula also is the one to use if you want to be able to finger press pattern pieces to the back.

Over the course of writing this book, I found that I never used the Matte formula of Mod Podge, because the Fabric and Gloss formulas had all the qualities I needed.

Please take special note that fabrics prepared with Gloss Mod Podge have a much stronger ability to bond to the background fabric. Once set with high heat, the appliqué is pretty much there to stay. Any attempt at removal will ruin the appliqué and stretch the background fabric. The bond created by using Gloss Mod Podge is even stronger than that of using fusible web. This leads to some very interesting possibilities. It is especially helpful for holding thin, delicate cutouts in place while you machine stitch them.

You can work around this super strong bond found in Gloss Mod Podge by first pressing the appliqué on using the lowest setting on your iron and holding the iron in place over each area for only 4 or 5 seconds. Repositioning appliqués will be easy and it will not damage the fabrics to do so. Once you are sure that you like what you see, set your iron on the highest setting recommended for your fabric and iron the appliqués on permanently.

Mod Podge versus White School Glue

Some of you may be wondering what makes using Mod Podge so different from using a white, liquid school glue, such as Elmer's. Mod Podge is not only a glue, but also a sealant. This gives it many different properties that make it perfect for iron on appliqué:

WHITE GLUE	MODGE PODGE
Soaks through fabric	Does not soak through quilting weight fabrics. It sometimes soaks through thin fabrics and a small patch should be tested first. Backcoating helps prevent this.
No adhesive properties once dry	Treated fabrics can be ironed onto other fabrics
Distorts fabric as it dries	Keeps your fabric looking nice
Can get messy	Since you can use it dried, it keeps your work mess-free
Paper patterns will not adhere to dried white glue.	Paper patterns are easily finger pressed or ironed on to treated fabric. They are also easily peeled off.
White glue dries faster so it is harder to get a smooth finish with it on your fabrics.	You can take the time to smooth out the Modge Podge as it takes longer to dry.

The Process

Tools and Supplies

This is a list of *helpful supplies* and tools shared by many of the projects. Each project will have a more specific list.

- Fabric for your project
- Plastic drop cloth or garbage bags
- Mod Podge
- Powdered white tempera paint (optional)
- Sponge brushes
- Transparent tape and Masking tape
- Iron and ironing board
- Pressing Sheet (freezer paper or a non-stick pressing sheet)
- Pressing cloth
- A small pair of scissors with a very sharp point
- A rotary cutter and cutting mat
- Matching cotton or cotton/poly threads
- Invisible thread (I like YLI Wonder size .004, in smoke and clear)
- Sewing machine needles in smallest size that will work with your thread and machine
- Presser foot with good visibility of the stitching area
- Straight stitch plate (if your machine is equipped with one)
- Sewing machine

For all the projects in this book, I worked with my 1956 Singer® 301A sewing machine, "Dorothy" (fig. 3). A Singer 301A only sews a straight stitch, but it does that one thing very well. You don't have to have a fancy sewing machine to do great appliqué.

Fig. 3. Singer 301A

Working with the Patterns

You will find the patterns for all the projects located at the end of this book. In order to use them, you will need to enlarge them as directed on a copier. You can take the book to an office supply store or print shop and they can copy the patterns on one sheet of paper. Copying it at home may require piecing it together and taping. Located on the copyright page are the permissions to copy/print only the pattern pages.

Here is an example (fig. 4) illustrating how to put the pattern pieces together:

Catmint Cottage is 16" wide. In order to get a life size pattern, the front face of it needs to be printed out across four 8½" x 11" pages.

Once you have the printouts, trim them before taping them together. For purposes of illustration I have lightly shaded the areas that should be trimmed off. In reality, you would line up your ruler along the edge of the printed image and trim off the excess margin.

Match up all the design elements and secure them with transparent tape. Viola! You now have a full size pattern.

The Process

Fig. 4. Assembling a pattern

Fabric Preparation

To pre-wash, or not to pre-wash, that is the question.

Many people never prewash fabrics and don't seem to have any problems with that. My personal experiences have taught me to prewash fabrics first if the finished item will ever be laundered. Fabrics shrink enough in the laundry that it might make appliqué work pucker. Even high quality fabrics will bleed a little dye into the wash water. I like to resolve all those potential troubles before I sew, rather than after I put in the time and effort to make something beautiful. In some instances in this book, you will be using iron-on products that specifically call for prewashing.

In most cases, if the finished project will never be laundered, there is no need to prewash the fabric.

Applying the Mod Podge

Start by laying out a plastic drop cloth of some kind to protect the work surface. I use garbage bags for this. When I'm through, we reuse them for trash, so there is no need to store sticky drop cloths. Lay out the fabric pieces (wrong side up!) on the work surface, in a way that makes them easy to reach.

It isn't often that the things we like best turn out to be the least expensive. The best tool I have found for applying Mod Podge is a sponge brush. They wash up easily and can be reused.

The Process

Mod Podge is a low fume product. Even so, it is always best to work in a well-ventilated area. When coating a lot of fabric pieces at once, you will definitely notice an odor. It goes away quickly as the pieces dry.

I find that Mod Podging fabric is a relaxing process (fig. 5). Put on some music and let your mind wander as you work.

Fig. 5. Applying Mod Podge to fabric

The first thing you should do is make a test swatch of your fabric and apply the Mod Podge of your choice. Sometimes, when a fabric has a more open weave, there will be areas where the Mod Podge leaks through to the right side of the fabric. This doesn't happen too often when you use the fabric formula, but it does sometimes happen when using the other two formulas. Pre-washing fabric makes it even less likely, because it tightens the weave.

It doesn't matter if the fabric is a little wrinkly, because the wrinkles will iron out later on. However, the fabric does need to be able to lay flat. You should iron out folds and ridges, because Mod Podge has a tendency to build up more in those areas.

Mod Podge is applied to the fabric before the appliqué is cut out. Using the sponge brush, apply an even, thin coat of Mod Podge over the surface of the fabric. It isn't necessary to coat the whole piece for large appliques. You can trace out an outline of the pattern on the wrong side of the fabric. Then, when you apply the Mod Podge, concentrate on the areas both inside and slightly over the edge of the appliqué piece's outline. In this example, the flowers were my pattern and they were large enough that I did not have to coat the centers (fig. 6).

Fig. 6. Front and back of fabric

With this fabric, LakeHouse DayZ Deux, you can see the design through the backside very well. This made it easy to apply the Mod Podge over the edges of the area I wished to cut out. In cases where you can't see the design, hold the fabric up to light and use pencil or chalk to mark the area where you want the Mod Podge applied.

Most of the time when I worked, I found I needed to coat a larger piece of fabric in its entirety. This is usually the case when the shapes you wish to cut out are small and/or close together or when you know you will be cutting many shapes, but you don't know their placement.

If you are coating the whole piece of fabric, work on a small section at a time. It is okay to get a little thick with your brush strokes, but keep in mind that any large drops or ridges should be brushed out as you work, because they will dry that way and cause a lump. So before you leave each section, feather the ridges out by holding your brush very lightly and whisking it over the area until it levels out and creates a smooth surface. Do not go over the areas too many times or use too much force with the brush. Doing so might force the Mod Podge through to the front of the fabric.

How Much is Just the Right Amount?

Be sure not to go overboard and apply too much Mod Podge. Also, be careful not to get Mod Podge on the right side of the fabric. I like to hold one side of the fabric piece down and brush the Mod Podge on in long stokes out toward the other side. The right amount should look opaque white when it is applied. It will turn clear as it dries (fig. 7). Humidity and temperature effect drying time. Generally, Mod Podge for Fabric should be dry to the touch in 30 minutes. It should look clear and be ready to use in about 45 minutes to an hour.

Once the Mod Podge is completely clear and dry, you are ready to go. Your fabric can be cut, ironed, and sewn. It won't be any trouble to stitch through the dried Mod Podge and it will not gum up your needle.

Special Fabric Treatments
Back-coating:

One very exciting thing I discovered about the Crafted Appliqué method is that it can be used to make thin and light colored fabrics more opaque, so that the background fabric will not show through. I did something that seems a little crazy that I call back-coating, which is actually applying paint to the back of the fabric. Back-coating makes light colored fabrics less transparent and keeps the appearance of colors more pure when the appliqué lies over a darker or patterned fabric background.

To Back-coat fabric, you will need the following supplies:
- Fabric or Gloss Mod Podge
- Powdered white tempera paint (I used Art-Time® by Sargent Art®)
- A small container with a lid for mixing and storing
- A small spatula
- Measuring cups and a measuring tablespoon
- Plastic drop cloth
- A sponge brush

Fig. 7. Wet and Dry Mod Podge

The Process

Make sure to always test out the process on a small sample of your fabric—every type of fabric is different and testing is a very important step.

First, decide whether you will need to use Fabric or Gloss Mod Podge. The Fabric one is better if the item will be laundered and the Gloss is better if you want a really strong bond between the appliqué and the background fabric.

There are two recipes, one for Fabric Mod Podge and one for Gloss Mod Podge.

Fabric Mod Podge/Paint mix
- ¼ cup of Fabric Mod Podge
- 1 to 2 tablespoons of powdered tempera paint. The amount depends on how much opacity you need.

Gloss Mod Podge/Paint mix
- ¼ cup of Gloss Mod Podge
- 2 to 3 tablespoons of powdered tempera paint. The amount depends on how much opacity you need.

Measure out the ingredients into a small container. Be careful with the tempera powder, because it might stain if it gets on your clothing, and for goodness sakes, don't sneeze. (Ask me how I know!)

Use a spatula to scrape the Mod Podge out of the measuring cup and very thoroughly stir the mixture. Now it is ready to use and may be applied in the same way you would apply the straight up Mod Podge.

One unexpected benefit, besides creating greater opacity, is that this technique makes the Mod Podge thicker, thus enabling its use on fabrics with a more open weave.

Back-coating the fabric like this does make it a little bit stiffer. This is something to keep in mind, because it might affect the outcome of the project. Some projects will be helped by added stiffness, while others will not.

> **Handy Hint:**
> When treating many pieces of fabric, they can be stacked after they have completely dried and any sticky edges trimmed away. The important thing is to make sure the Mod Podge sides are all facing the same direction with the Mod Podge side up against the plain fabric side of the next fabric piece.

Starching Background Fabric

I am a big fan of using starch for quilting. Fabric is a lot more cooperative and less apt to stretch out of shape when it is starched. There are a couple of projects in this book in which I recommend that the background fabric be quite heavily starched before applying the appliqués. This helps to minimize any stretching and distortion as you sew along the appliqués in every direction. The starch does not lessen the appliqués' ability to adhere.

This is how I heavily starch fabric:

Dip the background fabric in a dishpan full of pure liquid laundry starch. Make sure

The Process

the fabric gets completely saturated. Gently squeeze the fabric to remove the excess starch. Pour the leftover starch back into the jug to be used again.

Hang the fabric up and let it dry until it is barely damp (I hang it over the shower curtain rod). It is important to let starched fabrics dry almost all the way before ironing them, so you don't create starch frosting all over your fabric and make a mess of your iron.

Press the fabric, making sure to remove all the wrinkles. If your fabric dried completely before you had a chance to iron it, don't worry. Just lightly mist it with water before pressing.

The background fabric was as crispy as construction paper after I did this. I was worried about being able to maneuver the stiffened fabric under the throat of my sewing machine. Don't worry, the fabric will still scrunch and roll out of the way just fine. If it gets too soft from being squished up; just touch it up again with your iron.

Spoonflower® Fabric

There are two projects in this book for which I used fabrics purchased from Spoonflower, an online textile company that prints custom designs. I used Spoonflower fabric for three reasons: First, because I found wonderful fabric that I could not resist. Second, I wanted to highlight how fun and affordable it is to use unique and custom printed fabrics in our work. Lastly, the fabrics from Spoonflower will still be available after this book is published, thus making the project easier to recreate if you so choose.

For each project in this book, I have mentioned which fabric printing process I chose. A favorite of mine is Basic Cotton Ultra. The colors achieved with this are more vivid than most of the other printing processes. While slightly more expensive, Organic Cotton Sateen is also very good.

If you decide to order fabrics from Spoonflower, be aware that it can take up to two weeks before you receive the fabric, because it is printed on demand.

The Process

Stiff Stuff

For CATMINT COTTAGE and SUPER QUILTER, I used a product called Stiff Stuff by Lazy Girl Designs™. It is well named, being a firm yet flexible, sew-in interfacing. It has an amazing ability to bounce back into shape after being crushed. This is the product that enabled me to make CATMINT COTTAGE without having to create any sort of support structure for the walls and roof.

If you order Stiff Stuff online, it is better that you receive the product in a roll, instead of folded. Most companies will roll it for you if you write a note with your check out instructions. While Stiff Stuff usually bounces back, if it has been shipped or stored folded, it will have what seem like permanent creases. If it is heavily creased, all is not lost; Stiff Stuff can be easily repaired.

Cindy Foley, from Erica's Craft and Sewing Center, offered this advice:

> *To remove creases in Stiff Stuff, simply cover the area with a damp pressing cloth and steam iron it. If the creases are particularly tough to beat, dribble water along the crease and let it sit for a bit. Then cover it with a pressing cloth and steam iron it. Works like a charm!*

Laying out and Applying Appliqués

Laying out the appliqués for a simple design is very straightforward. For more complex projects, you should plot out and play with where you want the appliqués to be applied, before ironing them in place. They can, of course, be peeled off and repositioned if you change your mind.

Layering your appliqués adds depth to the way your project looks. If your project has more than three or four layers that overlap, you might find it better to stitch down the layers a few at a time. Otherwise, it is easier and works well to iron all the layers on and then stitch them all on in one go.

In the first photo (fig. 8), I used leaves cut out with an Accuquilt GO!® Baby fabric cutter. The Mod Podge prepared fabrics work very well with die cutters.

Once you have everything in position and are ready to iron on the appliqués, carefully cover the area with a pressing cloth (fig. 9). You could use a square from an old pillowcase, use freezer paper turned shiny side down, or a non-stick pressing sheet. This step is sometimes, but not always, needed to protect the surface of your iron, as well as to keep the appliqués from being scooted out of position. If the appliqué edges are cut cleanly with no Mod Podge showing, then your iron is usually safe. I have found sticky junk to be more of a problem when working with fusible web interfacing. If you ever do mess up the sole plate of your iron, wait until it is cool and then clean it with a Magic Eraser® sponge.

The Process

Fig. 8. Laying out the Appliqués

Fig. 9. Cover with a pressing cloth

Use as high a heat as your fabric allows. Steam is not necessary. Press one section at a time: lay the iron on the fabric and hold it there. I like to wiggle it a little to avoid iron marks, but don't iron back and forth. For the best results, press each section for 8 seconds. If you are like me, you rush through this when pressing. You will get a nice, strong hold with this amount of time.

Stitching Appliqués

For all of the projects in this book I used a simple straight stitch. For machine sewn appliqués, I think the straight stitched edge gives a tidier look and doesn't distract the eye from the image you are trying to create. With Crafted Appliqué, you don't need to worry about the edges fraying, so a straight stitch will do just fine.

Sometimes, I do what I call a hand turned wiggle stitch, which looks better when sewing along the edges of appliqués such as tiny florals, plant edges, fur, etc. By this I mean that I wiggle the piece back and forth as I go along. I use this technique when I need to create a more natural look with an outline that is not so sharply delineated. You might wonder how to do a wiggle stitch if your sewing machine only has a straight stitch. I do it on my Singer 301A by decreasing the presser foot pressure just a little bit, which allows for some wiggle room without lifting the foot. You can see a close up example of this in Catmint Cottage (fig. 16, p.75).

The Process

If your sewing machine has the capabilities, you can of course zigzag, satin stitch, or blanket stitch around the edges. It all depends upon the look you want. Once the appliqués are stitched down, you can also add any special touches with embroidery or beading.

Handy Dandy Implements

Use a presser foot with good visibility heading into the stitching point, with a clear view of where the needle enters the fabric. It does not necessarily have to be an open toe or embroidery foot. I bought a universal clear plastic foot for my machine.

Unless you are using a satin or any other kind of zigzag stitch, sew with a straight stitch plate in your machine. You can see that in my photo—the needle descends into a simple hole and not a slot. My Singer only does a straight stitch and so it has just that plate. If your machine has the option, use a straight stitch plate. It provides better support to the appliqué edges as you sew.

Use as small a size needle as you can for your thread and fabric. The smaller the needle, the smaller the holes it leaves behind. I normally use a Size 9 needle in my 301A. It takes a little experimentation and practice to see what works for you, your thread, and your machine.

When appliquéing, I favor using either invisible thread or matching thread. That way my imperfect stitching isn't so obvious.

If you have not used invisible thread before, or have tried it in the past and did not like it, now is the time to try again. Invisible thread is no longer the stiff and pokey fishing line of days gone past. Invisible thread comes in clear or dark colors and it is a visual chameleon, blending with the fabrics behind it. If you can find it, matte finish invisible thread shows up even less. Harriet Hargrave's own private label .004 Nylon by YLI™ was all the recommendation I needed!

When I am working with one color of appliqué, I often like using a matching cotton or cotton/poly thread. When sewing down appliqués of many different colors I prefer to use invisible thread. Otherwise, I would drive myself crazy with too frequent thread changes.

For the bobbin thread, choose a cotton or cotton/poly thread in a neutral color. If

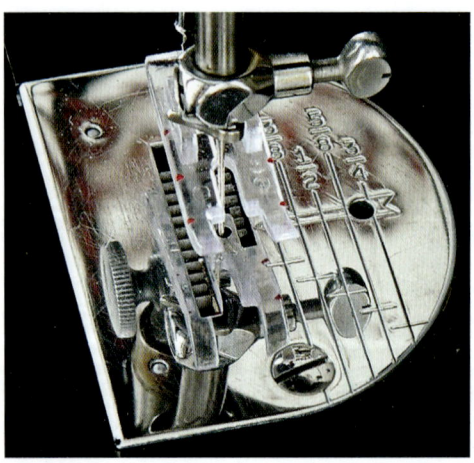

Fig. 10. A presser foot with good visibility. This is my favorite presser foot for appliqué.

you are working on a project that is already sandwiched with batting and backing, choose the predominant color of the backing fabric for the bobbin thread.

The main drawback in using invisible thread is that you will see the little pokey holes from your needle. Cotton or poly threads will fill up the holes, so they will be less noticeable. You will still need to use the smallest needle as possible.

Sometimes, for design purposes, you will want to use contrasting thread, such as in the veins of leaves. If you like contrasting thread, test a few different colors to determine which looks best.

Technique

I do have a lovely modern sewing machine with a speed control function. It strikes me funny that my old Singer seems to have better speed control. I think this is because once you become familiar with a sewing machine, it becomes a great partner. You learn just where all the sweet spots are when it comes to controlling the quality of your sewing. I found that I could do better appliqué work with my Singer 301A. I can tick-tick-tick along at any speed I choose and I choose "Slow." No matter what machine I sew on, if I try to go fast, I feel like I am on Mr. Toad's Wild Ride at Disneyland®.

Some people can sew accurately at higher speeds. Some can even stitch on appliqués by free motion quilting them. I am not one who can do that. In tight spots I will even hand turn the wheel until I am good to go again.

When sewing appliqués, it is best to plan ahead. Think of it like you would a road trip and look for areas you can hit along your route. Stitch in some of the details as you go along. Especially try to add in the details that won't be easy to reach later on.

If you have pieces that lay one over the other, it is not necessary to sew where they overlap. Your stitches will often add texture and dimension, so keep that in mind too. The areas along your sewing lines will be pulled down tighter against the background fabric and create the illusion that they sit further back.

Sometimes you will have to stitch over an area that you have already traveled before. Try to plan it out so that you never stitch down the same line more than twice. If need be, end that stitching line and start a new one in the place where you were headed.

Tips and Tricks

I am mostly a self-taught quilter, but I have learned a lot from reading great books and from joining The Quilting Board®, an online forum with members who love to share ideas and help each other out. I also learn a lot through experimentation, trial, and error. So I am going to share with you the tips that help me turn out a satisfactory project.

The Process

Three ways that I like to start and stop stitching lines are:

1. Make a few stitches in place at the beginning and end of each line of stitching to secure your threads.

2. Sew backwards for two or three stitches and at the beginning and end of each line of stitching.

3. Leave a tail of thread at the beginning and end of the stitching line. Then, when you have the fabric out from under the presser foot, turn it over and use the bobbin thread to pull the top thread through to the back of the fabric. Tie the two together in a knot. If you are working with just the top layer of your project, trim the tail to about a ½" long and you're done. If you already have your quilt sandwiched, pull the thread tails through a needle and then bury them in between the layers of your sandwich. Be careful about getting dark thread behind light sections of your top fabrics.

Stitch approximately 1/16" to 1/8" from the edge. Try to stay the same distance from the edge around the whole appliqué.

Use a shorter stitch length than you would for regular sewing. The smaller the appliqué is and the more complex its shape, the smaller you will want your stitch length to be. A shorter stitch length allows greater precision when sewing around tight curves and corners. It pays to experiment on a practice shape until you are happy with what you see.

As you stitch along curves, gradually turn your fabric so that the area where it reaches the needle is in clear view and straight ahead for the next stitch. Whenever all that turning causes the presser foot to pull or put a strain on the fabric, make sure that your needle is in the down position and lift the presser foot to adjust the fabric so that the next stitches lay straight ahead. When sewing along small curves you will need to repeat this process frequently.

With Crafted Appliqué, you can choose not to stitch around the edges of your appliqué. You can stitch to add detail. Or you can do both. If you do not sew around the edges, then it is good to sew the details right up to the edges wherever you would not want the appliqué to lift up.

As with everything: Practice makes perfect!

The Projects

CHUBBY CHECKERS
21" x 29"

 # Chubby Checkers
21" x 29"

Our family played a lot of checkers while the kids were growing up. So it comes as no surprise that one of the things I wanted to design for this book was a checkerboard quilt. It needed a theme, so I started looking at fabrics on Spoonflower for ideas. As soon as I saw Grace Felizardo's "Truffle Treats" fabric, the whole idea took on a life of its own. Since her free time was scarce, Grace sent me the hex (color) codes so that I could design a coordinating cupcake cup fabric. The two Spoonflower fabrics make a very nice pairing, since both have Grace's eye-catching color scheme. They look smashing against the dark, bittersweet chocolate colored background. It makes a fanciful table topper, but also is fun to play with. I used really big resin buttons for the checkers, which people find hard to resist.

Materials and Supplies

To be used in addition to the general Tools and Supplies list.

- 1 yard of background and binding fabric – I used Kona® Cotton Solid in Espresso.
- ½ yard of backing fabric – I used Alece Birnbach "Dessert Divas" Kisses in Brown for Robert Kaufman.
- ¼ yard of fabric 1 for checkerboard – I used Kona Cotton Solid in Red.
- ¼ yard of fabric 2 for checkerboard – I used Kona Cotton Solid in Pistachio.
- 1 fat quarter of candy fabric – I used "Truffle Treats" by Grace Felizardo, aka gracedesign of Spoonflower, and ordered it in Organic Cotton Sateen.
- 1 fat quarter of cupcake cup fabric – I used "Yum Ripple" by me, aka buzzinbumble of Spoonflower, and ordered it in Basic Cotton Ultra.
- ⅛ yard of fabric 1 for icing – I used Bake Sale Dots Yellow by Lori Holt of Bee in My Bonnet for Riley Blake Designs.
- ⅛ yard of fabric 2 for icing – I used Sprinkles in Dustberry, part of the Flower Fairies Collection of Alexander Henry.
- 8" x 10" fabric for cake – I used Kona cotton in Parfait.
- Batting – I used Hobbs 80/20.
- Perle Cotton thread (optional) – Cindy used DMC®.
- Gloss or Fabric Mod Podge
- White Tempera Paint Powder (if you would like to backcoat the fabric)
- Thread to match the appliqués
- 12 really big red buttons – 1½" is a nice size
- 12 really big brown buttons – 1½" is a nice size

Instructions

Using the Pattern

First, refer to (pp. 12–13) for printing instructions. Make five (5) copies of the full-size pattern (p. 82). Roughly cut out the paper patterns with at least a ¼" margin around each one. The final cutting will be done through both the paper pattern and the fabric, at the same time. If you are using the "Yum Ripple" fabric, then you do not need the cup pattern and can simply cut cupcake cups directly out of the Mod Podge treated fabric.

Fabric Preparation

I chose to backcoat the cupcake and truffle treat fabrics because they are resting on a very dark background which shows through them. You can read about how to do the backcoating technique in the section about Fabric Preparation (pp. 15–16). The fabric for the checkerboard, the brown background, and backing fabrics do not have to be treated.

Cutting Out the Appliqués

Place each pattern piece over its respective fabric. Cover with a pressing sheet. With your iron set on the lowest setting, very lightly press each part of the cupcake patterns to the treated side of the appliqué fabric. Let cool. Cut around each piece, just outside the edge of the black outline. Layer each cupcake cup/cake/icing unit on a pressing sheet and fuse together with a hot iron (fig. 1). Let cool and set aside.

Next, cut sixty (60) candies out of the "Truffle Treats" fabric, or other fabric. Cutting a few extra is a good idea too. Be sure to get a nice variety of shapes, colors and designs, and aim for the larger sized treats. Set these aside.

Fig. 1. Cupcake appliqués

Constructing the Checkerboard

Cut four 2½" x 21" strips of fabric 1 and four 2½" x 21" strips of fabric 2.

With right sides together, and using a ¼" seam, sew them together along their edges in alternating stripes. Turn to the wrong side and press all the seams in one direction (Diagram A, fig. 2).

Cut the striped piece into eight 2½" wide strips (Diagram B, fig. 2).

Lay the strips out in order and wrong side up. Flip every other one, end to end. The seams will now be facing in alternating directions and the squares will be in a checkered pattern (Diagram C, fig. 2).

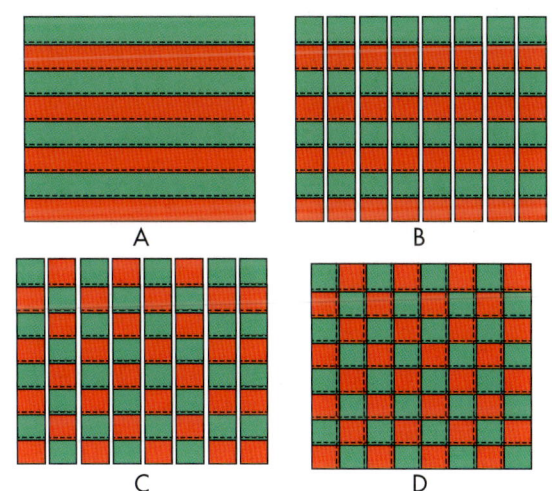

Fig. 2. Checkerboard construction

Chubby Checkers

Pick up strips 1 and 2. Place them right sides together, matching the seams by nestling them into each other. Clip or pin them together and then sew with a ¼" seam. Continue on, joining strip 2 to strip 3, and so on, until all 8 strips are sewn together into a checkerboard (Diagram D, fig. 2). Press the new set of seams open.

Cut two strips of fabric 3½" x 17½" and sew them to the sides of the checkerboard. Trim off their ends evenly with the top and bottom edges of the checkerboard, as indicated by the yellow lines (fig. 3).

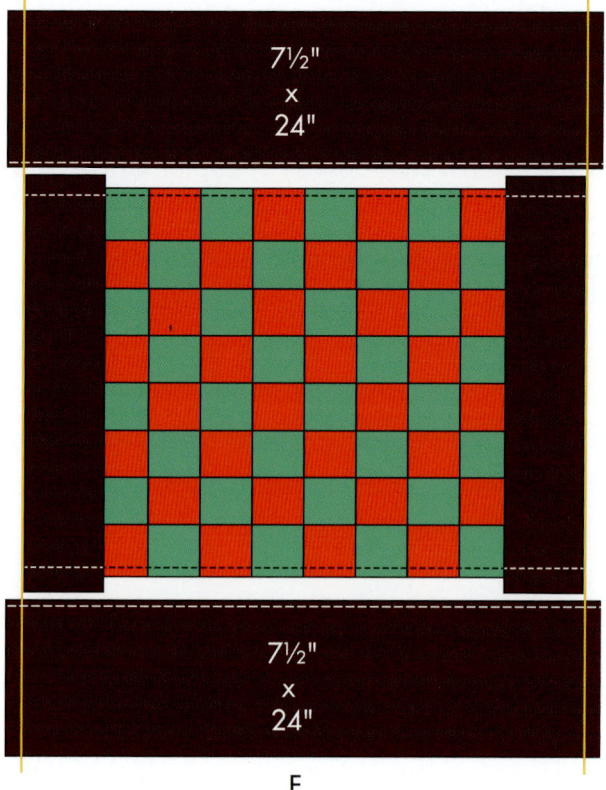

Fig. 4. Checkerboard construction

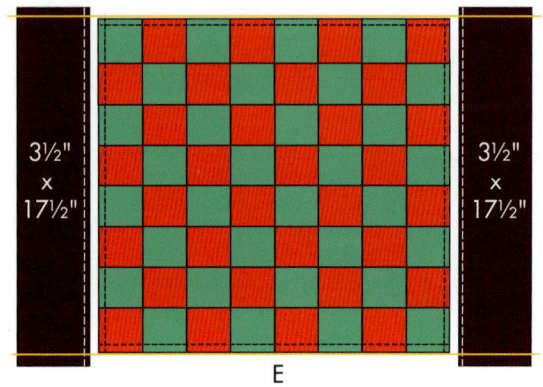

Fig. 3. Checkerboard construction

Cut two strips of fabric 7½" x 24" and sew them to the top and bottom of the checkerboard. Trim the ends of the top and bottom strips evenly with the sides, as indicated by the yellow lines (fig. 4). Square up the quilt top.

Ironing On and Stitching the Appliqués

Place five (5) cupcakes in a row across the top of the checkerboard and when you are happy with their positions, cover them with a pressing cloth and fuse them into place. Turn the checkerboard around and repeat the process across the bottom of the checkerboard. Refer to the photograph of the quilt for a placement guide.

When the cupcakes are all set, you can begin creating a border with the truffle treats. I found that it helped to work symmetrically, starting in the middle of the sides and ends and working out toward the corners. They should be ¾" away from the edge of the quilt top. Play with their placement until you are happy, then cover them with a pressing cloth and fuse them in place.

Your checkerboard quilt top is ready to sew. At this point, I chose to layer the quilt sandwich: top, batting and backing. This way, when I stitched on the appliqués, half the quilting was finished. You can also just work with the quilt top. Either way is good.

The first step, if you are working with the whole quilt and not just the top, is to stitch around the outside of the checkerboard squares as well as the outside of the whole piece with matching thread. This will hold everything in place nicely.

Before sewing on the appliqués, make sure that the machine is set up with top thread that matches the appliqué fabric and bobbin thread that matches the backing fabric, or use invisible thread. I used invisible thread around the truffle treats. Start and stop the sewing for each piece with a couple of back stitches, and then lift the needle and presser foot and move on to the next piece. You can trim off all the joining threads when you are finished.

Finishing

Quilt as desired. Those might be the three most frustrating words in quilting. Here is what I did in addition to the quilting already completed by sewing the appliqués:

I sewed around the red checkerboard squares with matching red thread. Then I bound the quilt, because the next thing I had in mind was to turn CHUBBY CHECKERS over to my sister-in-law, Cindy Buccella. She is accomplished with embroidery, among other things; the perfect person to do some big-stitch hand quilting around the truffle treat border. Cindy used dark brown perle cotton and did a wavy line of stitching that curves around the truffle treats. It looks like jimmy sprinkles—a very sweet finishing touch!

Fig. 5. Cindy's big stitch hand quilting

Designer Spotlight:
Grace Felizardo

"Truffle Treats' fabric started out as abstract doodles. I was experimenting with different shapes and thought they would make a nice abstract-geometric design for a fabric. I tried a number of color palettes which were not really working and was close to shelving the project but I persisted till I found the perfect colors. Well, those perfect colors made my shapes look like fancy truffles. It so happened that Spoonflower had just announced a 'sweets' design contest. So, I entered my 'abstract' fabric and called it 'Truffle Treats.' To my surprise, it placed second!"

Folk Art Christmas
18" x 27"

Folk art and quilting have many things in common. Both are often informally learned by observation, with ideas and techniques passed along from person to person. In fact, quilting can be a kind of folk art. Folk art is a very accessible form of creative expression and for that alone, I have always loved it.

This small quilt design combines elements of a few traditional folk art styles. Perhaps you can see the influence of Norwegian Rosemaling, Pennsylvania-Dutch, and Colonial American styles of folk art.

Materials and Supplies

To be used in addition to the general Tools and Supplies list.

- 1 yard of background fabric – I used Christmas Peace by Whistler Studios for Windham Fabrics # 35440B.
- 1 yard of backing and binding fabric – I used the same fabric as the front.
- ¼ yard of fabric for the appliqués – I used a Kona cotton solid in Snow.
- Batting – Valerie used Hobbs 80/20.
- Gloss Mod Podge
- Thread to match the appliqués
- Powdered white tempera paint (if you would like to backcoat the white fabric)
- Laundry or spray starch
- Pattern

Instructions

Using the Pattern

First, refer to (pp. 12–13) for printing instructions. Roughly cut out the paper patterns with at least a ¼" margin around each one (p. 83). The final cutting will be done through both the paper pattern and the fabric, at the same time.

Fabric Preparation

Heavily starch the background fabric before applying the appliqués. This helps minimize stretch and distortion as you sew along the appliqués in every direction.

As you probably know, most other fabrics show through white fabrics. I found that Kona cotton is better than most white fabrics in this regard. However, it is still fairly translucent when you put dark or patterned fabric behind it. To get around this problem, I used the back-coating technique on the white appliqué fabric. You can read about it in the section about Fabric Preparation (pp. 15–16).

Folk Art Christmas

For this project, I chose to work with Gloss Mod Podge because I wanted the bond between appliqué and backing fabric to be as strong as possible. I found that this formula works best to help the narrow stems stay in place as you stitch over them.

Cutting Out the Appliqués

With your iron set on the lowest setting, very lightly press each appliqué pattern to the treated side of the appliqué fabric. Let it cool. Cut around each piece, along the outside edge of the black outline.

Ironing On and Stitching the Appliqués

Peel off and place the appliqués onto the background fabric, referring to the layout diagram. Be very careful to make sure that they are facing coated side down.

> **Handy Hint:**
> You can choose to sew the appliqués on to the quilt top only, or you can layer the quilt sandwich and sew the appliqués on through all three layers. If you will be quilting the quilt on your home sewing machine, sewing the appliqués while the quilt is already sandwiched is a good way to start your quilting. I knew I would be sending my FOLK ART CHRISTMAS out to Valerie, so she could quilt it on her longarm sewing machine, so I chose to work only with the quilt top.

With Gloss Mod Podge, you must initially work with your iron set on the lowest setting and only lightly fuse on the appliqués. If necessary, reposition the appliqué pieces until you have the desired layout. Once you are happy with the way everything looks, then go ahead and lay your pressing cloth over the whole project and fuse the appliqués to the fabric with the iron set on high heat.

Now the quilt top is ready to take to the sewing machine. I prefer to use matching thread rather than invisible thread, because it helps fill the needle holes.

For each appliqué piece, start and stop your stitching by leaving a long tail of top and bobbin threads. Pull these through to the back of the quilt as you work, to be hidden later. It makes for a very neat and tidy looking front.

Fig. 1. The appliqués before stitching

My daughter Alina agreed to try sewing this quilt. She is a beginner and had never sewn curves before. She completed the whole lower half of FOLK ART CHRISTMAS in one sitting. She worked slowly and didn't rush herself and found that this helped her to be very accurate with her stitching. I was very happy she could make part of this quilt.

Finishing

Square up and trim the quilt top. Make sure to get the tree upright and centered, so that the quilt will look balanced. Stay stitch ⅛" along the outside edge of the background fabric. Layer the backing, batting and quilt top into a quilt sandwich. Quilt as desired and then bind.

Valerie's quilting is so intricate and amazing! She did very small McTavishing style quilting all around the appliqués, which echoed the shapes in both the appliques and the background fabric. The quilt turned out gorgeous!

Fig. 2. Close up of Valerie's quilting

Quilter Spotlight:
Valerie Smith

Valerie is a longarm quilter and textile artist based out of northeast Ohio where she lives with her husband and four children. She's been machine quilting for over a decade on a domestic machine, but in 2013 purchased an APQS longarm quilting machine. Since that time, with hours of hard work and dedication, she has built a successful business focused on hand guided custom machine quilting, quilt pattern, and pantograph design.

Valerie's quilt designs have been featured in some of the top Quilting magazines on the market such as Quilts and More Magazine and Modern Quilting Unlimited. Independently, she has self-published two educational books used in conjunction with hands on teaching and lecture, four original quilt patterns, and co-designed over a dozen pantograph quilting patterns for Urban Elementz.

Specializing in complicated custom quilt design that often takes hundreds of hours to complete, Valerie's work has received various ribbons and awards on the regional as well as national level. Her goal is to combine a love for traditional quilting with a unique artistic perspective. To see her latest works visit her website at

www.pumpkinpatchquilter.com.

The Walking Tree
28¼" x 28¼"

The Walking Tree was inspired by the walking trees in C.S. Lewis' Chronicles of Narnia, which were trees with spirits. The pattern is designed to be the centerpiece for a sampler quilt. It also looks lovely on its own and would make a wonderful signature or family tree quilt. It's the perfect quilt for using up scraps too.

Materials and Supplies

To be used in addition to the general Tools and Supplies list.

For my appliqués I used fabrics from Howard Marcus' Collections for a Cause: Love, Friendship, Warmth, and Comfort as well as 3 Sisters "Double Chocolat." All the leaves came from scraps of these fabrics.

You will need
- 1 yard of background fabric – I used Indigo Crossing by Minick and Simpson for Moda 14752 in Ivory.
- ¾ yard for the trunk – If your fabric does not have a directional print, you can use a fat quarter, with the trunk laid sideways
- 3 or more charm packs, or enough scraps to make 182 leaves – The Walking Tree leaves can be entirely made up of leftover scraps.
- Fabric Mod Podge (have a second jar on hand in case you run out)
- Laundry or spray starch
- Freezer paper
- Top thread (I used YLI Invisible thread in Smoke)
- Bobbin thread to match the background
- Transparent tape and masking tape
- Pattern

Using the Pattern

First, refer to (pp. 12–13) for printing instructions. I preferred to make two full sized patterns, one for cutting and one for checking the layout. The Walking Tree pattern is found on p. 84.

Fabric Preparation

Choose fabrics for the leaves and trunk that have enough contrast with your background fabric. Coat the back of the fabrics that will make up the tree's leaves and trunk with Fabric Mod Podge. Let dry.

Heavily starch the background fabric before applying the appliqués. This helps minimize stretch and distortion as you sew

The Walking Tree

along the appliqués in every direction. The starch did not lessen the leaves ability to adhere well before they were stitched in place.

For more detailed instructions on how I starch my fabric visit the Fabric Preparation section (pp. 16-17).

Cutting Out the Appliqués

Carefully cut the tree's trunk out, leaving the main paper pattern intact.

Flip the tree's trunk pattern over, so that it is a mirror image, and place it in position on the back of the treated trunk fabric. Lay a piece of freezer paper, shiny side down, over the area you will iron. Press the trunk fabric, trunk pattern, freezer paper sandwich together, holding the iron over each area for 8–10 seconds. Remove the freezer paper.

Cut around the tree trunk, just on the outside edge of the black outline. Leave the paper pattern in place.

Before you cut out the leaf patterns, position, iron, and sew the tree trunk appliqué to the backing fabric, referring to steps 1–6 in the ironing and stitching guidelines in the next section (pp. 35–36).

For the leaf patterns, carefully cut them out without disturbing the background paper. Leave a little margin of white around each leaf. They are symmetrical, so there is no need to flip them over to mirror image. In fact, you want those numbers to show.

I have color coded the leaves into 4 groups. If you are using a variety of fabrics, you can choose to use this as a guide so that the colors are dispersed in a pleasing arrangement around the tree (fig. 2).

Firmly finger press each paper leaf pattern onto the back of its fabric. If many leaves share the same fabric, feel free to move the patterns fairly close together.

Cut around each leaf, just on the outside edge of the black outline. Leave the paper patterns in place.

Ironing On and Stitching the Appliqués

While designing this pattern, I found that it really does matter what sizes the leaves are and how they are positioned around the tree. I created several mock ups before I found an arrangement that I liked. I wanted The Walking Tree's leaves and branches to have a sense of movement, as if they were playing with the wind.

If you would like to try a little improvisation, you can do this, too. Have some fun playing around with arrangements. Or, if you prefer, you can approximate where the leaves go by using the photograph of The Walking Tree as a guide (p. 32). In my case, when it came time to iron the leaves and tree trunk onto the background fabric, I wanted to follow the pattern as exactly as possible.

There is a reason I said to cut the trunk and leaf shapes out carefully, leaving the background intact. If you do this, The

THE WALKING TREE

WALKING TREE pattern will now act as a large template with open windows where the trunk and leaves belong. This is a very helpful template to have if you want the same layout as shown.

It isn't completely necessary, but it helps to have a second printed full size pattern, or you can use the pattern shown in this book as a placement guide as you plan your colors and iron on the shapes. You can place the corresponding leaf number on the pattern, as you cut, to also use as a placement guide.

For the tree trunk

1. Place THE WALKING TREE template right side up on the background fabric. Make sure the template is lined up diagonally and centered and that it lays flat and perfectly square.

2. Carefully peel off the paper pattern backing from the tree trunk. At this stage, the tree trunk is somewhat gangly and awkward.

Fig. 2. Color coded diagram of THE WALKING TREE

The Walking Tree

3. Position the tree trunk appliqué, treated side down, in the template window.

4. Use the tip of your iron to tack the trunk in place on the background fabric.

5. Remove the template. Fuse the tree trunk to the background fabric by pressing it, section by section, for 8–10 seconds.

6. Stitch the tree trunk in place.

For the leaves

1. It helps to work in smaller batches, because you will be manipulating the fabric a great deal as you sew the leaves onto the background. I worked with 45 leaves at a time.

2. Each time you are ready to position a set of leaves, place the template over the background fabric, lining it carefully up over the tree trunk. Use masking tape around the edges to hold the template in place.

3. Working one leaf at a time, peel off the paper pattern backing and lay the leaf by number inside the corresponding window left by the cutout. Make sure each leaf is set in with the treated side down.

4. Use the tip of your iron to tack each leaf in place.

5. Once you have a set of leaves positioned, lift off the template and fuse the leaves in place, pressing each area with your iron for 10 seconds.

6. Stitch each batch of leaves in place.

7. Repeat the process until all the leaves are appliquéd. It goes a lot quicker than you would think.

My choice was to avoid having stitches running from leaf to leaf. In order to do this, I stopped and started the stitching at the base of each leaf with two or three back and forth stitches, and then hopped over to the next leaf without cutting the threads.

After every two or three leaves, trim off the joining threads on top. You can trim all the bobbin threads at once when you finish the tree. Unless you have eagle vision, it would be very hard not to miss some of those invisible thread links on the top of the quilt.

With all that turning around, it is pretty easy to get mixed up and have trouble keeping track of which leaves you've already sewn. My solution was to place small stickers on the latest row of leaves, moving them as I went along (fig.3).

It is pretty relaxing to feel yourself get into a rhythm as you move around the tree. Before you know it, you will have something very exciting taking shape beneath your hands!

Fig. 3. Using stickers to keep track of where you've already sewn when using invisible thread.

Finishing

When THE WALKING TREE is completely appliquéd, place the template one last time over the top of the centerpiece. Mark the corners of the 27" square and remove the template. This is not going to be a perfect square, but it gives you an idea of where to start. You can tweak the size of the panel to fit your needs.

From corner to corner, measure diagonally across the square, centering the line through the tree trunk and mark the two points. Make sure to get the tree upright and centered, so that the quilt will look balanced. Repeat this again on the two opposite corners, measuring the same distance and marking the two points. Mark the edges of THE WALKING TREE panel. Now make sure that the panel is perfectly square. (It will be turned 45 degrees, forming an on-point diamond.)

The panel is designed to be 27½". If you plan to use it as a sampler quilt centerpiece, add a slightly larger than normal seam allowance. It can always be trimmed later. Carefully cut out the panel with its seam allowance.

Stay stitch, ⅛" along the outside edge.

Quilting can take place when the rest of the sampler is done. However, if you are making THE WALKING TREE as a stand-alone quilt, then it is now ready to be sandwiched, quilted and bound.

I asked my friend Julie to quilt THE WALKING TREE for me. We decided it would look wonderful if her quilting added visually to the sense of movement in the tree, like a breeze swirling around the branches. Julie flew with this idea. She created a freestyle, swirling pattern that almost looks like post-impressionistic painting. Her beautiful quilting adds so much life to the tree.

Quilter Spotlight: Julie DeGrave

Julie lives with her husband on 33 acres of heavily wooded property in the hills of Holland, New York. This mother of 2 received her first sewing machine at the age of 10 and has been sewing in some capacity ever since. Quilting first found its way into her life in the form of a "Lone Star". This pattern has led to a 20 year love affair (some might call it an obsession) with fabric and quilt designs. In 2010, with an empty nest approaching, Julie decided to go to the next level. She purchased an APQS Millennium Longarm, and Pines and Needles Longarm Quilting was officially off and stitching. Busy from day one, Julie has enjoyed the relationships that she has developed with her customers and their own passion for quilting, while at the same time creating a new obsession list to be conquered, pre cuts, threads, edge to edge designs, rulers, batting, etc. Because, according to Julie, "One can never have too much!"

You can contact Julie at: www.pinesandneedlesquilting@gmail.com

Cecropia Utopia
18" Pillow

Moths have always been fascinating to me. Perhaps, because they are nocturnal, they seem almost otherworldly. It takes a little more effort to find them than it does with brightly colored butterflies. They sometimes come in fantastic disguises, blending in perfectly with tree bark and lichen. Many moths are even somewhat drab in appearance, unless you look at them closely. There are some moths, like the Cecropia, that are so beautiful they take your breath away.

I made the Cecropia moth pattern for this pillow much larger than life. For my moth, I chose to use Oakshott Cottons. The visual texture of these fabrics does a very good job of imitating the frosted and velvety appearance of the moth's wings

Materials and Supplies

To be used in addition to the general Tools and Supplies list.

- 1 yard of background fabric – I used a medium weight cotton duck fabric called Air Traffic, Felix Aviation for Premier Prints in natural/pewter.

- 1/16 to 1/8 of a yard of each of the fabrics shown in fig. 1, p.40. Descriptions of color are very subjective, so I made a Fabric Swatch List, showing the fabrics I used and the amount you need to treat with Mod Podge. I hope the swatch list will aid you in choosing fabrics.

- 1 yard of fusible fleece, OR 1 yard of woven fusible interfacing – I used Face-It Soft by Lazy Girl Designs, a lightweight woven 100% cotton fusible interfacing. You should choose which type of product to use by how much loft you want. The fleece will give the pillow a more quilted look. Both will reinforce the fabric and make for a sharper looking pillow.

- 18" pillow insert

- 12" to 14" zipper

- Fabric Mod Podge

- Powdered white tempera paint

- Matching threads

- One skein of embroidery floss – I used DMC 844, an olive grey color.

- Pattern

Cecropia Utopia

Fig. 1. Oakshot Cottons colors and corresponding pattern pieces

1. Oakshott Cottons Lipari – 15 Basiluzzo (9½" x 6") Pattern Pieces: 6, 8, 9, 10, 11, 12, 15,16, 17, 22, & 25

2. Oakshott Cottons Lipari – 01 Pollara (9½" x 15") Pattern Pieces: 1 & 20

3. Oakshott Cottons Colourshott – 01 White Sand (5" x 6") Pattern Pieces: 3, 7, 19, 24, 27, 29 & 30

4. Oakshott Cottons Lipari – 11 Lisca (9½" x 6") Pattern Pieces: 14, 18, 26, & 32

5. Oakshott Cottons Lipari – 11 Lisca (9½" x 6") Pattern Pieces: 14, 18, 26, & 32

6. Oakshott Cottons Lipari – 12 Stromboli (9½" x 6") Pattern Piece: 23

7. Oakshott Cottons Lipari – 10 Dattilo (9½" x 6") Pattern Pieces: 5, 13, & 28

8. Oakshott Cottons Lipari – 09 Lentia (9½" x 6") Pattern Pieces: 4 & 31

9. Oakshott Cottons Elements Earth – 22 Millstone (5" x 6") Pattern Piece: 2

Instructions

Using the Pattern

First, refer to (pp.12-13) for printing instructions. The pattern is located on (p. 85).

Fabric Preparation

If you have chosen to work with Oakshott cotton, which often has a more open weave, make sure you do a test swatch of the fabric before coating the whole piece. My suggestion is to prewash the fabrics, to help tighten up the weave.

Coat the back of the fabrics for the moth with Mod Podge. I used Fabric Mod Podge on my Oakshott Cottons and it did pretty well, with only a few small areas where the Mod Podge bled through to the other side of the fabric. Use a light hand when applying the Mod Podge and do not repeatedly go over the same areas. Back-coat the white fabric, as described in the section on Fabric Preparation (pp. 15-16). It is well worth going through all this because shot cotton frays easily and the Crafted Appliqué technique prevents the fraying.

The pillow panels will be sewn together with ⅝" seam allowances. That would add 10/8 of an inch to each dimension for the pillow panel, but I round the number down to 8/8 of an inch, for a tighter fit. This means that you should add 1" to the dimensions listed for your pillow form and that will give you the size you need for the front and back fabric panels.

Assuming you are working with an 18" square pillow form, cut two 19" squares of background fabric. Then cut two 19" squares of the fusible interfacing or fleece. Turn the background fabric panels over to the wrong side and fuse the interfacing (or fleece) to the back.

Cutting Out and Fusing the Appliqués

Roughly cut each paper pattern out, leaving a small margin of white around each one.

Using the Fabric Swatch List (fig. 1) and the Assembly Diagrams in figs. 2, 3, 4, and 5 (p. 42) as a reference, place the pattern pieces on the treated side of their respective fabrics and lightly iron them in place. If you used shot cotton, be aware that the fabric looks different depending upon from which direction it is viewed. With any directional fabric, you should take care to place the pattern pieces so that their mirror image partner is oriented in the same direction.

Cut around each shape and leave the paper patterns adhered to the back of the fabric until you are ready to use it.

Each pattern not only has the pattern pieces, but also an assembly diagram. As I built each wing, I cut out sections of the assembly diagrams to use as a template and placement guide.

Transfer the pieces to your ironing board. It works best to build each wing and the body separately on a pressing sheet, rather than trying to start the shapes directly on the pillow front. Once each wing is assembled, cover it with a pressing cloth and fuse it into one piece with your iron.

When you have all four wings and the moth's body assembled and fused, layer them

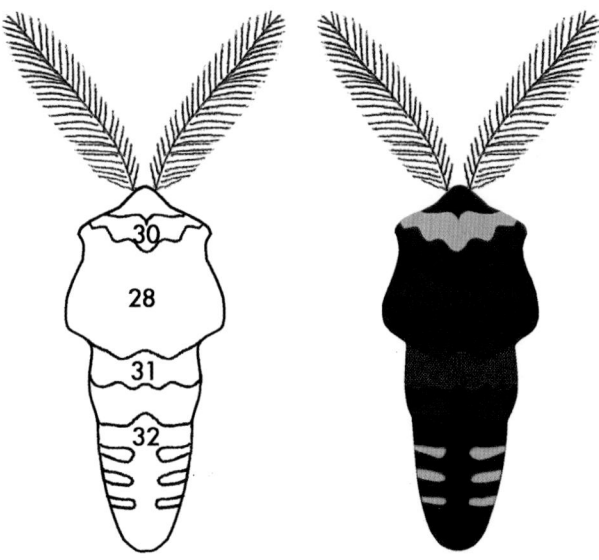

Fig. 2. Diagram of assembled moth body

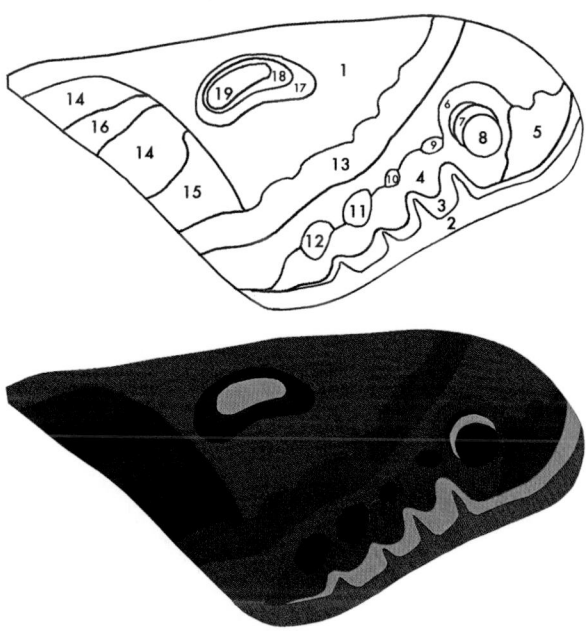

Fig. 3. Diagram of assembled upper wing

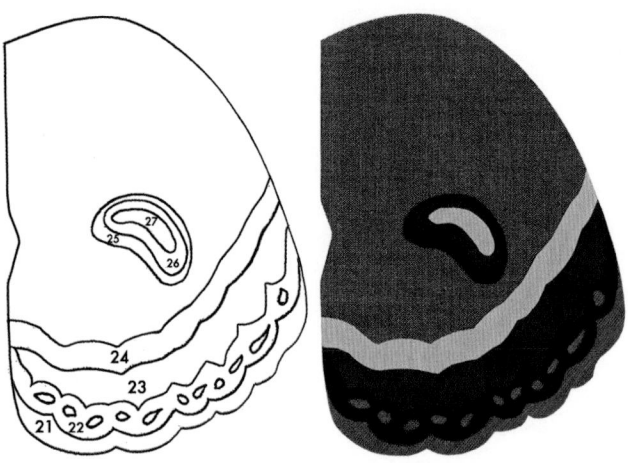

Fig. 4. Diagram of assembled lower wing

Fig. 5. Assembled moth

together as shown in fig. 5, (p. 42). Cover with a pressing cloth and fuse. Your moth is ready for appliquéing.

Stitching the Appliqués

When the moth is fully assembled, position it on the front pillow panel. It helps to place it a little higher than center, because pillows tend to slump down over time and that way the moth will remain completely visible. I turned my moth at an angle, to give it a more lively appearance.

Stitch along each color of fabric with matching or invisible thread. I used matching thread and changed colors as I went, hiding and tying off the tails of the thread on the back side of the panel. It doesn't take long before the appliqués are completely stitched in place.

Embroider the moth's antennae, using the pattern as a guide.

I chose to count the appliqué work as the quilting. You can, if you prefer, add more quilting at this time.

Assembly and Finishing

Ever since my first zipper sewing attempt in 4-H Club with the ever patient Mrs. Starowitz, zippers and I have not been on friendly terms. Much to her dismay, I sewed the zipper to both the front and the back of the dress simultaneously. It is best to follow the installation instructions that came with your zipper.

- Install the zipper on the bottom of the back and front pillow panels.
- Fold the panels, right sides together and line up the sides and top edges.
- Make sure the zipper is open. Pin or clip the panel edges together.
- Starting where the zipper left off, sew along the bottom, up around a side, across the top, down the next side and back to the other end of the zipper.
- Trim off the corners of the seam allowances and turn the pillow cover right side out.
- Use a tool to work the corners and sides out into nice sharp lines. Press.
- Stuff the pillow form into the cover and zip the cover shut.

It's Super Quilter!
Sewing Machine Needle Case and Patty Cake Cats pincushion made by Kait Buccella

It's Super Quilter!
Sewing Machine Needle Case
15¼" x 11"

When we were brainstorming about projects for this book, my daughter Kait came up with the idea for this needle case. Since one of the things I wanted to do was test the Crafted Appliqué method with beginners, I thought it was only fitting that Kait be the one to make this project. She is relatively new to sewing and recently made her very first quilt. I am tickled pink that she is getting the sewing bug.

Most needle cases are made for hand sewing, but we thought it would be useful if this one also held sewing machine needles. You can customize the case to fit your own personal sewing needs. This one is set up with needles for Kait's Singer Featherweight.

Materials and Supplies

To be used in addition to the general Tools and Supplies list.

- 1 fat quarter for the outside of the case – Kait used "Rainy & Criminal Night" by Demigoutte (Virginie Ozanon) on Spoonflower. I ordered one yard of the fabric in Organic Cotton Sateen, so we could choose our scene freely. This fabric printed up with great color and I love Virginie's design so much that the extra fabric will not go to waste.
- 1 fat quarter for the inside of the case and for the windowpanes – Kait used Kona cotton solid in Fog.
- 8" x 10" red fabric for the telephone box – Kait used Kona cotton solid in Cardinal
- 1 sheet of felt – 12" x 18" – Kait used a wool blend in cream
- 1 sheet of inkjet printable fabric
- 1 yard Fusible web interfacing – Kait used Fusi-bond: lite
- 1 yard of Stiff Stuff – Lazy Girl Designs
- 1 piece of clear vinyl, 12" x 18"
- Fabric or Gloss Mod Podge
- ⅝" Heavy Duty Snap Fastener & Setting tool
- Matching threads
- Blue painter's tape (1" or 2" width)
- Fabri-Tac Permanent Adhesive (optional)
- Pattern

Instructions
Using the Pattern

First, refer to (pp. 12–13) for printing instructions. You will find the pattern for It's Super Quilter! on (p. 86). There is also a page

IT'S SUPER QUILTER

for the telephone box sign and needle size labels. The label page is designed so that you can print it out on inkjet fabric.

Scan the telephone box label patterns into your computer. You can then edit this in a photo or paint program. We tried to provide a lot of variety when I designed the label page and had a little fun with the signs for the telephone box. If you will be using any of the signs and needle labels, print the label page onto inkjet printable fabric.

Fabric Preparation

Prepare the red fabric for the telephone box with either Gloss or Fabric Mod Podge. Kait noticed that we can see a little shadow of the background fabric showing through the red, so you might want to try the back-coating technique on this fabric (pp. 15–16). The telephone box sign and a rectangle of the fabric for the window panes are better if they are back-coated.

Cutting Out the Appliqués

Roughly cut out around the paper pattern for the telephone box. With your iron on the lowest setting, very lightly press the pattern onto the treated side of the red fabric. (Be sure to protect the iron with a pressing sheet.) Let the fabric cool and then cut out around the perimeter of the box, along the outer edge of the black line. Do not peel the pattern off until you have decided how you will cut out the window panes.

I experimented with two ways to do the windowpanes (fig. 1) and found that my favorite way is to actually cut out the telephone box window grilles (method 1). This is how we did our project. Try a little test to see which method you like best.

Method 1: You will need the paper pattern to still be adhered to the back of the telephone box for this method. Work on the pattern side. Use the sharp point of your scissors to poke a hole in the center of each pane and then carefully cut out a circle around the hole. From there you can trim around the straight lines of the window grille. Cut out

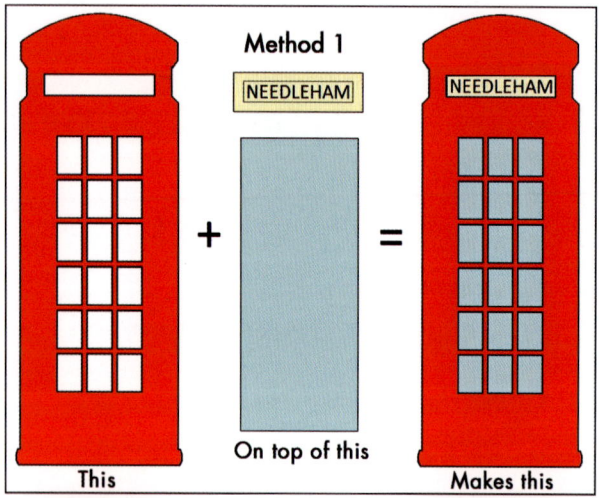
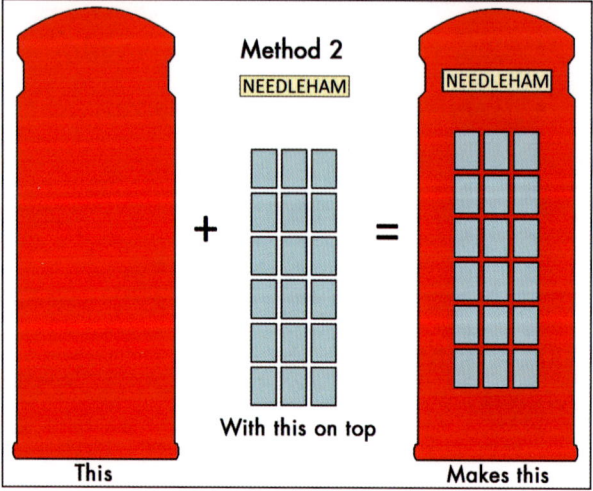

Fig. 1. Two methods for cutting windows

Crafted Appliqué: New Possibilities · · · · · Lara Buccella

all the grilles, being careful not to cut too far. On a pressing sheet, center the red telephone box over a rectangular piece of the treated windowpane fabric and iron the two pieces together. (Both pieces should have their treated sides facing down.)

Method 2: Leave the telephone box whole. Remove the pattern from the back. Use the pattern over again and apply it to the back of some treated windowpane fabric. Cut out all the window panes. Place them in position on the telephone box and lightly fuse in place. Make adjustments if needed and then fuse with your iron on high heat.

The sign for the telephone box can be applied in either of these ways as well. Once you have built the telephone box on your pressing sheet, let it cool and then peel it off and set it aside.

Creating the Exterior and Interior of the Needle Case

Cut panels from the Stiff Stuff in these sizes:

For the exterior of the case:
- Two pieces 7½" x 11" (Exterior Front and Exterior Back Panels)
- One piece ⅜" x 11" (Exterior Spine)

For the interior of the case:
- Two pieces 7¼" x 10¾" (Interior Front and Interior Back Panels)
- One piece ¼" x 10¾" (Interior Spine)

It is very important to make sure that you keep the Exterior and Interior pieces separated and do not mix them up.

Iron fusible web interfacing to the wrong side of the exterior and interior fabrics. Let the fabrics cool and then peel away the paper backings. Make sure to save this paper because it makes a wonderful pressing sheet.

For the Outside of the Needle Case

If your fabric for the outside of the needle case is a larger print like ours, then you will want to position it so it makes a nice scene with the telephone box on the front of the case. You do this by placing the Exterior Front Panel on the wrong side of the fabric, behind the part of the scene you are interested in. At the same time, check to make sure there is enough room for the Spine and Exterior Back Panel, which will sit to the right of that, as well as for 1" of fabric extending past the Stiff Stuff Panels all the way around (fig. 2).

Position the Stiff Stuff panels and fuse them one at a time. First put the front panel in position on the wrong side of the fabric. Lay a pressing sheet over it and fuse it from the Stiff Stuff side. Then flip it over, place it on top of a pressing sheet and fuse it from the fabric side. Next, place the spine in position, ¹⁄₁₆"

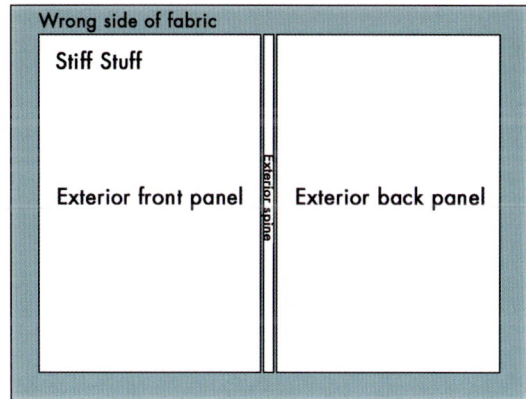

Fig. 2. Fusing the panels to the exterior fabric

It's Super Quilter

away from the front panel and fuse that from both sides. Last of all, place the back panel 1/16" away from the spine and fuse that in place from both sides (fig. 2).

Now it is time to fold the extra 1" of fabric around the edges of the Stiff Stuff (fig. 3).

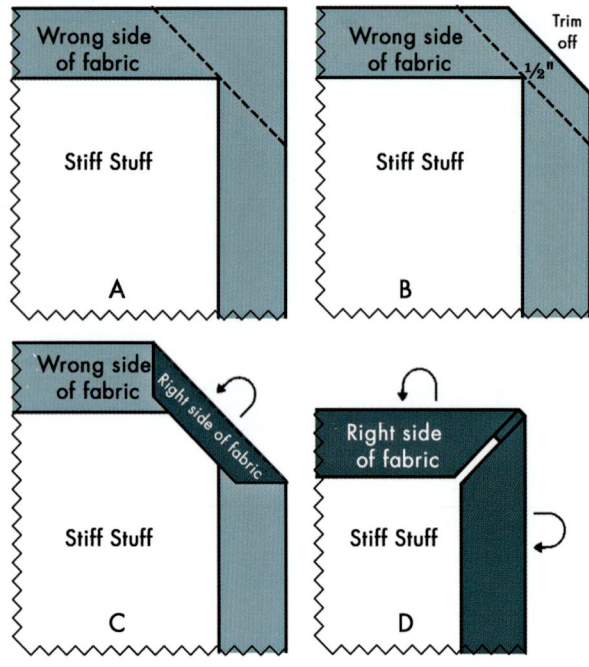

Fig. 3. Creating neat corners

To create a neat corner with no frayed threads sticking out:
- Fold the corner over the Stiff Stuff at a 45 degree angle and crease it.
- Trim off the tip of the corner, leaving ½" of fabric.
- Fold the corner back over the Stiff Stuff, cover it with a pressing sheet and fuse it in place. Iron on a ½" strip of fusible web across the top of the folded corner (where diagram C says "right side of fabric"). This will help hold the sides on where the fabric was folded.

- Repeat these steps with the other three corners.
- Fold a side flap snuggly over the edge of the Stiff Stuff. Fuse the side neatly in place. Repeat for the other three sides.

The corners come out slightly squared off with this method, which will help keep them from curling and being bent with use. Figure 4 shows the case exterior after the corners and sides have been fused around the edges of the Stiff Stuff.

Fig. 4. Assembling the exterior of the case

For the Inside of the Needle Case

Repeat this same process with the interior panels and fabric. Be very careful when you wrap the fabric around the Stiff Stuff panel edges. It needs to be snug up against the edge, but not so tight that it bends the edge in. This should create a slightly smaller version of the case exterior.

The interior is ready to be customized with pockets and felt to hold your needles.

- Lay your needle packets (and any other items you wish the case to hold) directly on the case interior in a pleasing arrangement. Don't crowd the items in too close together. You should allow room in the vinyl pockets for the thickness of the packets.

- Plan an area or two for felt, which will hold single needles.

- Figure out if you would like to add labels and plan for those too.

- Measure each area where you would like vinyl or felt. The vinyl can be cut in 7" strips, because you will create divides for the pockets with stitching. Cut each section. It helps to use a rotary cutter and mat to keep everything straight. To keep the vinyl from slipping as you cut it, hold down one edge with blue painter's tape.

- Lay the vinyl strips on the case interior one at a time. Hold each one in place with painter's tape placed across the top. It is difficult to see the clear edge of the vinyl while you are sewing. We found that it also helped to place strips of tape butted up along the edges of the vinyl.

- Stitching about ⅛" from the edge, sew down one side, across the bottom and then up the other side of each strip. Remove the tape. Check to make sure everything is going to fit well.

- Sew on the other vinyl strips in the same way. When they are all in place, stitch lines across the strips for the pocket divides.

- Sew the felt squares in place.

- Sew on the labels for the needle sizes and any other customizations.

You can load the pockets up at this point and make sure that you are happy with everything. Then empty it all out for the next stages.

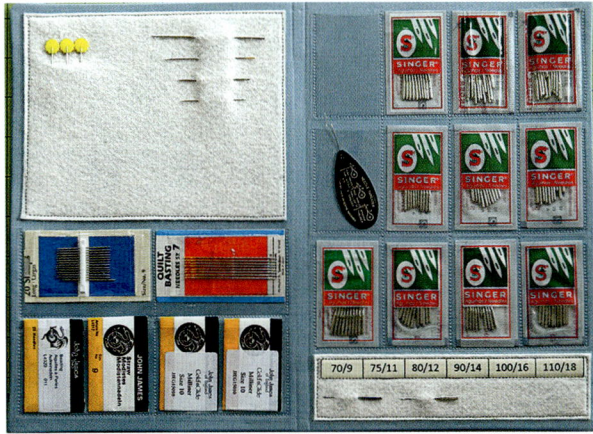

Fig. 5. The case interior

For our needle case, we set the pockets up on the right side to hold packs of 2020 Singer Sewing Machine needles for Kait's Featherweight. Then we put a used car lot at the bottom for needles that still have some mileage left in them. The needle size labels indicate parking spaces that will help her remember what size the needles are.

We set the left side up for hand stitching items, with pockets for the needle packs and a felt pad to hold more pins and needles.

Ironing On and Stitching the Appliqué

Lay the case exterior right side up. Place the telephone box so that it sits in the bottom right corner of the case front. Place a pressing cloth

It's Super Quilter

Fig. 6. Sewing on the appliqué

over the appliqué and fuse it in place. You can see that Kait set up the case exterior so that the spine rests right behind the road and there is a fun scene all around the appliqué.

To stitch on the telephone box, sew around the outside edge of the appliqué with matching red thread. Then change to black thread and, using the original pattern as a reference, stitch lines around the appliqué for the box's features, as shown on the pattern.

You can call the exterior finished at this point, or you could add quilting to the scene. We did very simple outline quilting around some of the printed elements in Virginie's wonderful fabric.

While sewing the appliqué and quilting, you may sometimes have to bend the panels to fit them under the throat of your sewing machine. They will develop creases. Do not worry that the creases are permanent. That is the beauty of using Stiff Stuff. When you are finished with the exterior, place it on your ironing board, cover it with a pressing cloth and steam iron the piece. The creases will disappear.

Do not do this with the case interior because you might damage the vinyl. Instead, work around the piece in such a way that you do not have to bend it.

Adding the Tab and Snap Closure

We decided to add a snap closure to the needle case. If you would like to make one, it is surprisingly simple to do. It's fun too, because you get to pound things with a hammer.

- Cut the tab pattern out in both the exterior and the interior fabrics.
- Place them right sides together and sew around the sides and curved end. Leave the straight cut end open. Trim the seam and clip the curves. Turn the tab right side out and press.
- Using the tab pattern, cut a slightly smaller tab out of Stiff Stuff. Insert the Stiff Stuff tab into the fabric tab.
- Follow the directions on the package for your snaps. Add the top part of a snap to the curved end of the tab. Make sure the exterior fabric will be facing out.
- Add the bottom part of the snap to the back panel of the case exterior. Make sure the right side is facing out and position the snap halfway along the case edge, no closer than ¾" from the edge.

- Snap the two parts together. Close the needle case exterior and bend the tab around so that it lies neatly over the front of the case. Mark where the tab meets the front of the case on both the tab and the case.

Flip the case exterior over so that it is lying wrong side up. Position the tab, wrong side up, using your marks as a guide. Hold it in place temporarily with a little bit of glue. Do not put any glue within ½" of the edge (fig. 7). The tab will be held between the exterior and interior in the next stages.

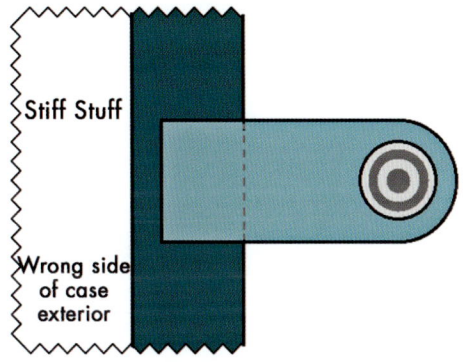

Fig. 7. Positioning the snap tab

Assembling the Needle Case

Now everything is ready to join the interior and the exterior of the needle case together. This can be accomplished by sewing or gluing them together. You can also combine gluing and sewing. The choice should be made after reading this next section.

If you choose to use glue, it is important to make a couple of test swatches of vinyl sewn over Stiff Stuff. Then test what happens when you glue two swatches, wrong sides together. Some glues react with vinyl and the fumes cause it to swell or bubble. I did a test with Fabri-Tac Permanent Adhesive, which creates a very fast and strong bond. It caused the vinyl to puff up a little bit, but it flattened out again by itself after the glue dried and it looked good as new. Your vinyl might be different than the one we used, so that is why testing is important. Also, always bear in mind that the glue will squish out a little bit, so you should not glue too close to edges.

If you choose to sew, it is a good idea to test out one corner to see if your sewing machine has the chops. There are a lot of layers to be sewn through all at one time, especially at the corners. Some sewing machines might have a difficult time in these areas and might skip stitches. Other machines will have no trouble.

We chose to glue the needle case because it held so well and looked so nice on the outside of the case.

In either situation, you must line up the spines first. Place the needle case exterior on your work surface, wrong side up. Now lay the case interior over it, right side up. Center it carefully, lining up the two spines. It should be slightly smaller so there is roughly ⅛" all the way around it. Pin or glue the spines together.

Glue method

- Place the case on the work surface so that the inside is facing up. Flip one of the interior panels over to the opposite side. Spread a thin layer of glue on the wrong side, being careful not to get too close to the edges.

- Press the panel down onto its corresponding side of the case exterior.

- Before the glue has a chance to set, lift the unglued side of the case so that it is up in the air at a 90° angle, as shown in fig. 8. It must stay in this position while the glue sets up. There is a reason for securing the sides while they are in this position. It is to prevent either side from warping as the other pulls on it when the case is lying flat or closed.

- Smooth the glued side down with your hand. Check to make sure there are not any glue bloops. If there are, clean them up. Smooth the glued side with your hands again and hold it in place until the glue has a good, firm grip.

- Repeat this same procedure for the other side of the needle case.

- Set up the case to dry by propping it in the position shown in fig. 9.

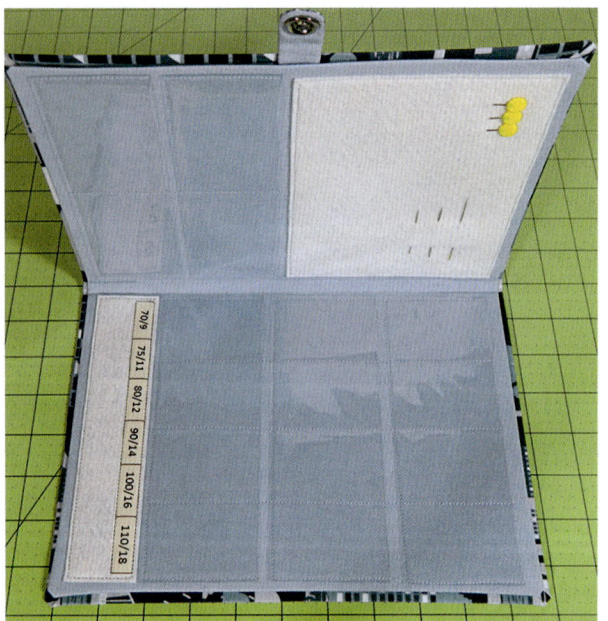

Fig. 8. Side is held at a 90° angle to the other

Fig. 9. Setting the case up to dry

It's Super Quilter

Sewing method

- After the case spines have been securely joined, lay it flat on your work surface.

- Working on one side at a time, raise one side up at a 90° angle. Use clips or pins along the edges to hold the interior and exterior panels together.

- Sew along the exterior, through both the interior and exterior panels, ¼" away from the edge.

- Repeat this same procedure for the other side.

Finishing

Once the glue is completely dry (it is best to wait overnight), or the sides have been sewn together, it is ready to use. Load it up with your needles and you are good to go!

Fig. 10. It's Super Quilter

Designer Spotlight:
Virginie Ozanon

Virginie wrote:

"I am a French print designer who dreams to open an e-shop providing stationery and decoration accessories. I'm very active on Spoonflower and I often take part on pattern contest. It's a huge community where I met a lot of talented designers.

I created Rainy and Criminal Night design for a Film Noir design challenge. I drew my inspiration from classic icons like buildings in the dark, intriguing ambiance, cigarette smoke, old cars and gangsters."

Virginie has a wonderful blog that you might like to check out, demigoutte.blogspot.fr.

Lara Buccella ····**Crafted Appliqué:** New Possibilities

HELLO, MR. RANGER, SIR!
Insulated Pic-a-nic Bag

Crafted Appliqué: New Possibilities · · · · Lara Buccella

Hello, Mr. Ranger, Sir!

Insulated Pic-a-nic Bag
16½" x 17½" x 6½"

One of my favorite cartoons has always been Yogi Bear. Even as a child, I was fascinated by the background scenery, just as much as by the shenanigans of Yogi, Boo Boo, and Mr. Ranger.

When creating a background for this vintage Shasta trailer appliqué, I wanted to imitate that style. It was hard work, but I forced myself to spend hours closely studying Yogi Bear cartoons. I decided to use solid color fabrics with little or no quilting after appliquéing. I wanted to give it a stylistically flat appearance, so it would look more like an early cartoon (fig. 1).

Now remember, "This is one project where it is okay to make a Boo Boo!"

Fig. 1. Setting the scene

Materials and Supplies

To be used in addition to the general Tools and Supplies list.

This design uses small amounts of many different fabrics. Think of it as using your fabrics like a paint box. The smallest size I have designated here is 9" x 10", or 1/16 of a yard.

- 1 yard of fabric for the bag body – I used Kona Cotton Spruce 1361.
- 2 yards of fabric for the tuckable bag lining – I used Pam Kitty Picnic, Recipe for Success from LakeHouse Dry Goods Fabrics.
- ½ yard fabric for the sky – I used Kona Cotton Orchid 1266.
- ½ yard fabric for the ground – I used Kona Cotton Fog 444.
- ½ yard of fabric for the bag bottom – I used Kona Cotton Espresso 1136, covered with iron-on vinyl. I would recommend using a ready-made brown vinyl fabric or laminated cotton
- ¼ yard of Kona Cotton Leaf 28
- ¼ yard Kona Cotton Shale 456
- 18" x 10" Kona Cotton Turquoise 1376
- 18" x 10" Kona Cotton Sage 1321
- 18" x 10" Kona Cotton Pewter 1470

Hello, Mr. Ranger, Sir!

- 9" x 10" Kona Cotton Charcoal 1071
- 9" x 10" Kona Cotton Everglade 356
- 9" x 10" Kona Cotton Forest 1145
- 9" x 10" Kona Cotton Glacier 146
- 9" x 10" Kona Cotton Graphite 295
- 9" x 10" Kona Cotton Holly 1161
- 9" x 10" Kona Cotton Iron 408
- 9" x 10" Kona Cotton Windsor 1389
- 9" x 10" Kona Cotton Teal 1373
- 9" x 10" of cream fabric for the Shasta – I used Pindot Ice Cream by American Jane for Moda.
- 9" x 10" of red fabric for the Shasta – I used Red Pindot by American Jane for Moda.
- Red floral fabric scraps for the Shasta awning, curtains and tires – I used two from Storybook Classics by Windham Fabrics.
- Insul-Bright or other insulated lining. You will need enough for two 24" x 28" rectangles. Insul-Bright is a heat reflective, insulating lining, perfect for a picnic bag.
- 2 yards of fusible or sew-in fleece, for added structure and insulation. I used Dreamy Fleece Fusible by Lazy Girl Designs
- 4 yards of light weight fusible web interfacing. I used Fusi-Bond Lite by Lazy Girl Designs.
- Adjustable purse shoulder strap with hooks
- Two D-rings (to match hook hardware)
- Cheap plastic placemat (optional)
- ½ yard of Iron-on vinyl (optional if using plain cotton) or ½ yard of ready-made vinyl or laminated cotton for the bag bottom. Ready-made is easiest.
- Pattern

Instructions

Using the Pattern

First, refer to (pp. 12–13) for printing instructions. Once you have the pages printed out, trim them and tape the sections together, if needed, for a full size pattern (pp. 87–91).

Fabric Preparation

Since the appliqués for this bag are mainly created with Kona cotton solids, which are slightly thinner fabrics, I recommend that you use the Fabric formula of Mod Podge. I also used the back coating technique (p. 15–16) for the lightest colored fabrics.

Cutting Out the Appliqués

Place each appliqué piece onto the treated side of the appropriate fabrics and lightly fuse in place with either finger pressing or an iron set on low. Cut each piece out and set aside. I prefer to peel off the paper pattern just before I am ready to place the appliqués in position. That way I don't lose track of which piece is which.

Ironing On the Appliqués

Prepare the background for the scenery panel by sewing together two strips of fabric for the ground (Kona Fog) and sky (Kona Orchid) as shown in fig. 2.

Hello, Mr. Ranger, Sir!

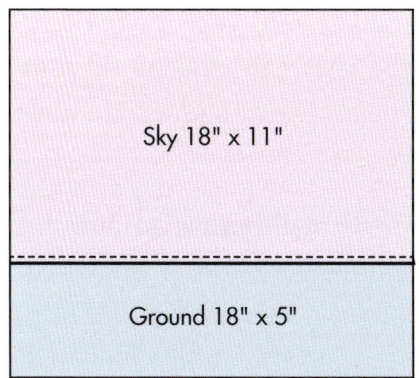

Fig. 2. The background for the scenery.

Create the large evergreen in the foreground by building the layers on a pressing sheet and then lift it off as one piece. Place it on the scenery and lightly fuse in place.

Fig. 3. Layout the pine boughs on a pressing sheet

These measurements include a ⅜" seam allowance. It is sized larger than needed to allow for squaring up the panel background after you sew the pieces together. Once it is sewn together, trim the scenery panel to a 13½" x 16½" rectangle, with the seam laying 4" up from the bottom.

On a separate note, each appliqué that sits along a panel edge already has a seam allowance added to the side that meets the panel edge. This way it can be sewn into the seams along the edge. Place any pieces like this just ⅛" away from the edge.

To assemble the appliqués, start with the first layer of mountains and iron them in place onto the sky/ground background. Next add the shadows and highlights to the mountains. After the mountains are in place, lay out all the rest of the appliqués, working your way forward in the scenery. Use the layer numbers on the patterns and the photo of the scenery as a guide.

Use a pressing cloth between the fabrics and your iron. This protects the appliqués and it also prevents a shiny ridge from being formed wherever seams and edges lay under the fabrics.

Build the Shasta trailer (fig. 4, p. 58) separately on the pressing sheet.
- Start with the white body of the trailer
- Add the red side panel.
- Build the tire by layering the grey circle (Kona Shale) on top of the red circle, on top of the black circle (Kona Graphite). Tuck it under the bottom edge of the wheel well.
- Build the door by starting with the grey rectangle (Kona Shale) and adding on the window pane (Kona Fog) and red side panel. Make sure that the red side panel on the door lines up exactly

Lara Buccella · · · · · **Crafted Appliqué:** New Possibilities

Hello, Mr. Ranger, Sir!

with the red side panel on the trailer body. Add the red awning. I created a little fringe for the awning by fraying the edge of untreated matching fabric and then trimming it and tucking it under the awning's lower edge.

- Build the window in the same way.
- Tuck the trailer hitch and propane tank under the front edge of the Shasta.
- Add the wing and the Shasta is finished. Place it in position on the scenery (fig. 5).

Fig. 4. The Shasta trailer

Fig. 5. The scenery panel

Once you have everything where you like it, fuse the layers in place with your iron set on high heat. The appliqués are not sewn on at this time.

Create a small border around the scenery panel by sewing 1" wide strips of contrasting fabric along the top and bottom of the panel, and then along the sides. Trim the corners even. For this, I used Kona cotton in Leaf.

Creating the Front and Back Panels

Use ⅜" seams throughout construction of the bag for added durability. Each time you sew fabric strips together, be sure to press the seams open between steps.

The diagram in fig. 6 shows what the front panel should look like once sewn and trimmed. (The measurements for cutting the fabric strips are on p. 59.) The pieces will be sewn together and trimmed, so you don't have to be too fiendish for accuracy here. What will be important is that the back and front panels align exactly with each other and I'll be explaining how to trim the back panel down to match.

This bag is constructed in such a way that there are no separate side panels—they are a part of the front and back panels. The light grey crisscross lines (A, B, C, & D on fig. 6) represent where the bag edges will be folded to form the top edge, sides, and bottom.

I used Kona cotton in Spruce for the body of the pic-a-nic bag. For the footed bag bottom, I used Kona cotton in Espresso and laminated it with iron-on vinyl before sewing. I found that the iron-on vinyl created extra work, because it frequently needed to be touched up. That being said, it does look really nice. I might try ready-made vinyl or laminated cotton next time. Each of these products needs to be protected from direct contact with the iron, a step you must never forget, which does make things interesting. Of course, you can use regular cotton for the bag bottom instead.

Cut the fabric strips to create the back and front panels as follows:

Spruce – bag body:
- (1) 4" x 19" strip
- (1) 3" x 19" strip
- (2) 6" x 18" strips
- (1) 20" x 28" piece

Espresso – bag bottom:
- (2) 6" x 28" strips

Front Panel Assembly

Sew the 4" x 19" strip along the top of the scenery panel.

Sew the 3" x 19" strip along the bottom of the scenery panel.

Cut off the ends of the top and bottom strips so that they are even with the side edges of the panel.

Sew each 6" x 18" strip to the sides of the scenery panel.

Cut off the ends of the side strips so that

Fig. 6. Front panel construction

they are even with the top and bottom edges of the panel.

Measure a level line 1½" below the bottom edge of the small Leaf colored inner border. Trim off the excess fabric along this line, across the width of the panel bottom.

Sew one 6" x 28" strip in Espresso to the bottom of the panel. Trim it even with the sides of the panel.

Measure 2½" up from the top edge of the small Leaf colored inner border. Trim off the excess fabric along this line, across the width of the panel top.

Back Panel Assembly

Sew the remaining 6" x 28" strip of Espresso fabric to the 20" x 28" piece of Spruce fabric, matching edges along the 28" length. Press the seam open.

Measure 17" up from the seam between

the bag bottom and body. Trim off the excess fabric along this line, across the width of the panel top.

Backing the Panels

Cut two 24" x 28" rectangular pieces of Insul-Bright batting. Set aside.

For each panel, flip it to the wrong side and carefully press the seams flat. Apply fusible web interfacing to the wrong side of the panel. Let cool and then peel off the paper. Save that paper—makes a great pressing sheet.

Lay the panel, right side up and centered onto an Insul-Bright piece. Move the panel so that it overhangs the Insul-Bright by 1½" along the top edge. (See fold over line A in the diagram in fig. 6, p. 59.) Make extra sure that the edge is evenly parallel with the rest of the panel.

Place a pressing sheet under this overhanging piece. Now, place a pressing cloth over the top of the panel and fuse the panel to the Insul-Bright.

Flip the panel over to the Insul-Bright side and fold the top overhanging flap (A) around the edge. Fuse it in place.

Trimming the Layered Panels

Use the top turned edge as the guide for squaring up the panel.

The sides of the front panel should be trimmed so that they extend 4½" past the outer edges of the small Leaf colored border. The bag width should be about 26" wide.

The bottom strip for the bag bottom should be trimmed so that it is 5" deep.

Now lay the fully trimmed front panel on top of the back panel, exactly aligning the tops of the panels and the seams between the bottom and body. Trim the back panel to match the front panel.

Sewing the Appliqués and Quilting the Panels

Carry the front panel to your sewing machine. Start by doing stitch-in-the-ditch along the insides of the small inner border. To secure the appliquéd scene, sew along all the exposed raw edges of each appliqué. I prefer to use threads in matching colors for this project. You can also use invisible thread. Instead of backstitching as you start and stop each line of stitching, leave a tail of thread. Whenever opportunity arises, pull the top thread through to the back of the panel and tie it in a triple knot with the bottom thread. Then trim off to only a ½" tail. You should do this fairly regularly so that you do not inadvertently sew over the tail threads.

I chose not to add extra quilting to the scene because I wanted to keep the appearance as flat and simple as possible. The appliquéing acts as quilting because it is sewn through the Insul-Bright. If you would like to add quilted details, now is the time to do so.

To Mark Off and Quilt the Panels

Stitch along the side fold lines (B and C on the diagram in fig. 6, p. 59). Please note that if you used vinyl or laminated fabric for the bag bottom, you should not continue the stitching line down onto the bag bottom fabric. Stop at the seam between the bottom and body. These fold lines should be 3⅜" away from the side edges of the panels.

Next, flip the panel over. On each side, make a small ½" snip in the top flap just on the outside of the lines you just sewed. Peel the flap up and secure it out of the way with tape. This way it will stay free for later when you sew the panels together (fig. 7).

Fig. 7. Pull aside the top flap

Sew a quilting line about 1" below the top of the panel. On the front panel, this line should meet up naturally with the top edge of the small inner border. Measure how far this is from the edge and duplicate it on the back panel.

Now you are ready to lay out the quilting lines. I chose a simple grid pattern, marked off with ¾" painter's tape. Start with the vertical lines first. Place the first piece of tape along the outside edges of lines B and C. Lay another piece of tape right alongside that one and so on. Remove every other line of tape and reuse it as you go along. Once all the tape is in place, stitch along the edges to create the vertical quilting lines. Do not sew the lines past the bag body into the vinyl bag bottom. Also, do not sew the lines into the top borderline (fig. 8 and 9).

Repeat this process for the horizontal quilting lines. It is the horizontal lines that have to meet up when you join the front and back panels, so be very accurate in how you place the tape.

Fig. 8. Taping the quilt lines

Fig. 9 Quilted lines

Assembling the Bag Exterior

Lay the front and back panels, right sides together. Line them up so that the top edges meet and the seams between the bag bottoms and bodies meet. Use clips or pins to hold the panels together. Lift up the top flaps you loosened earlier. Align them and sew them as part of the side seam. Sew around the sides and bottom, ⅜" from the edge.

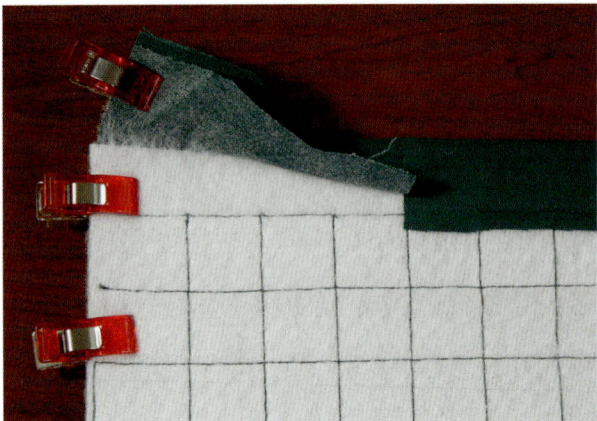

Fig. 10. Clipping the sides and flaps together

So, how does this flat-as-a-pancake creation become a three dimensional bag? This part is really a fun transformation: you make a boxed bottom.

To Make a Boxed Bottom

Open the bag, but keep it wrong side out. Flatten one of the bottom corners into a triangle and match up the bottom seam with the side seam. Place a long straight pin right through the centers of both seam lines to keep this position.

At the tip of the corner, draw a 6" line, at a right angle with the seam. Make sure that the seam line runs through the center point of the line, at 3". Sew along the line. Remove the pin.

Trim off the corner, ½" away from the 6" line.

Repeat these steps for the other corner.

Turn the bag right side out and press open the seams. Don't forget to protect the vinyl if need be.

At the side seams, turn the top flap over toward the inside of the bag and fuse it once again to the Insul-Bright.

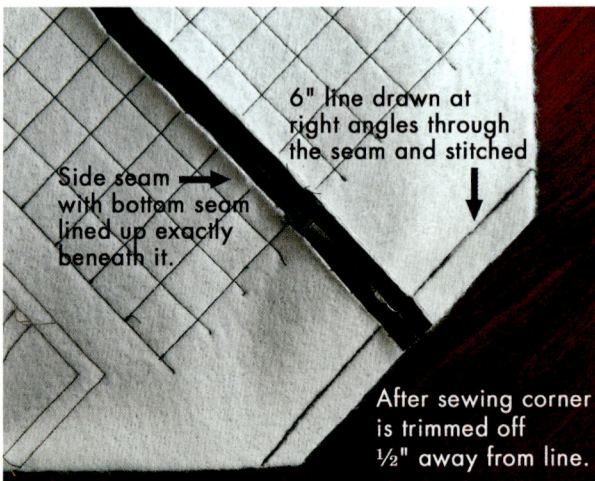

Fig. 11. Creating the boxed corner

Making the Strap Loops

Next it is time to add loops to the sides of the bag to hold the D-rings, so your strap can be hooked onto the bag. Refer to diagrams 1–4 in fig. 12.

- Measure the width of the D-rings you plan to use. Mine are 1½" across the bottom—the straight part of the "D."

- Cut a strip of fabric for the loop. The strip should be 14" long and 4 times the width of the D-ring. So, for a 1½" D-ring, that is 6".

- Fold the strip of fabric in half lengthwise

and right side out and press (Diagram 1, fold line 1). Next, fold the edges of the strip in to meet the middle and press (fold lines 2 and 3).

- Cut a strip of fleece or batting just a hair less than ½ the width of your strip and 14" long. Open the pressed fabric strip and lay the batting down the middle, between fold lines 2 and 3.
- Next, fold flaps A and B over the fleece and press (Diagram 3).
- Fold the strip in half lengthwise again, wrong sides together. Press it nice and flat. It should fit in the D-ring and be 14" long.
- Top stitch along the long edges of the strap to hold it together. If you wish to, add a second line of top stitching ⅛" in from the first (Diagram 4 – top).
- Cut the strap into two 7" straps (Diagram 4 – bottom).

Feed a 7" strap through a D-ring and pin the ends together onto the inside of the bag, centered on a side seam. Leave about 1½" of the strap, along with the D-ring, standing up above the edge of the bag. Sew the strap to the bag. For this, I like to use a stitching pattern that looks like a big X in a box. Repeat these steps for the other D-Ring.

Sewing the Bag Lining

The lining for Hello Mr. Ranger, sir! is expandable. It can be pulled up like a turtleneck collar and tucked in over the top of your pic-a-nic bag goodies.

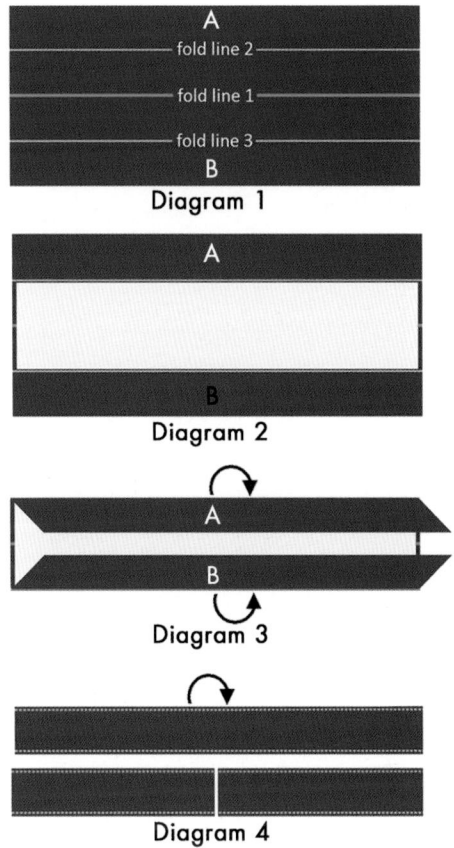

Fig. 12. Constructing the strap loops

Cut two panels of lining fabric.

Since my lining fabric has a directional print, I cut the fabric in two separate pieces and sewed them together, turned in opposite directions. That means, the 8" collar facing will look upside down. (Fig. 13, p. 64), but the print will be right side up inside the bag, as well as on the outside when the collar of the expandable lining is standing up or tucked over the contents of the bag.

If your lining fabric is not a directional print, then there is no need to make a separate collar facing. Just cut the two panels 34" x 24½".

Cut two panels of fleece or batting 26"x 24½". Either use fusible fleece or apply fusible web to the back of the lining panel.

Hello, Mr. Ranger, Sir!

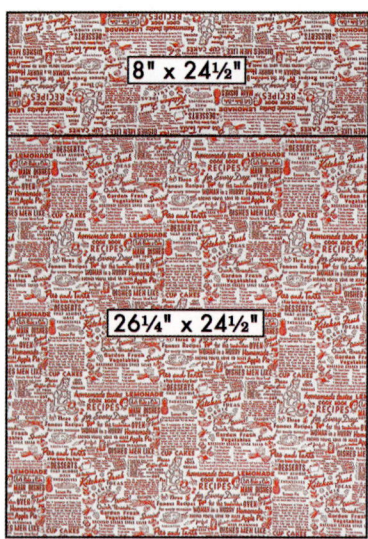

Fig. 13. One lining panel

Lay the fleece on the wrong side of each lining panel. Make sure that it sits on the bottom of the lining panel, just under the seam line between the 8" facing and the 26¼" pieces. Fuse in place.

Lay the two lining panels, right sides together and match up the side seams all the way to the top of the 8" flaps. Sew along the sides and bottoms of the two panels. Press the seams open.

Turn the 8" collar facing over to the wrong side of the lining. Pin in place and topstitch along the open, upper edge of the lining.

Sew a boxed bottom on the lining, just like you did for the bag exterior.

Leave the lining inside out. Fold the top of the lining insert over 6" and press with your iron to create a reference line.

If you wish, you can add a bit more structure to the bag bottom. An inexpensive way to do this is to cut a plastic placemat to fit and insert it into the bottom, between the bag outside and the lining.

Drop the lining, wrong side out, into the bag exterior. Make sure the collar is standing up straight, with the facing laying down nice and flat. Match the side seams of the lining and bag exterior. Match the reference line you just pressed to the border line you previously sewed on the bag exterior, 1" down from the top.

Pin in place on the outside of the bag, through all the layers.

Set up your sewing machine so that the bobbin thread matches the bag lining and the top thread matches the bag exterior. Stitch in the ditch, through all the layers, right along the 1" border line.

Finishing up

Tidy up the bag, pressing where needed and molding it back into shape. Attach the adjustable bag strap to the D-rings and HELLO MR. RANGER, SIR! is ready for many pic-a-nics to come!

Fig. 14. The tuckable lining

Catmint Cottage
Sewing Machine Cover

Lara Buccella · · · · **Crafted Appliqué:** New Possibilities · 65 ·

Catmint Cottage

Sewing Machine Cover
14½" x 16" x 8"

A lot of us are attracted to little houses. It's their unpretentious charm and cozy appeal that draws us in. I thought it would be fun to use architectural and landscape fabrics to make a sweet little cottage sewing machine cover. This is definitely a case of the fabric inspiring the creation.

Planning your cottage

Landscape and architectural fabrics are easy to find. If you can't track down what you have in mind locally, there are treasure troves of fabric sources out there on the internet.

The cottage would look terrific done up in other ways as well. Can you just see it as a gingerbread cottage made with graham cracker brown siding and candy themed fabrics? You could also make a toy store … or a pet shop … or give your imagination free reign and create a fantastical house. Perhaps a lair for a sleeping dragon?

If you decide to plant a garden around your cottage, look for a fabric (or fabric line) with florals that have depth, with highlights and shadows. Stylized or flat flowers would look nice too, creating an entirely different look.

It is also fun to experiment with the scale or size of the "plants" you use in the garden. Very small flowers will make the cottage look larger and grander. Oversized flowers will give the cottage a diminutive and magical look. This would be great with a cottage with stone walls and give it the feeling of a fairy cottage set in amongst the flowers. Flowers scaled to fit the size of the cottage give it a more lifelike look. When "planting" a cottage garden, layer your flowers and plants like you would see in a real garden, with the taller plants in the back and the little ones in the front. While the flowers don't really stick out past the edges of the cottage, one eye-fooling trick is to continue the planting around the corner. For a true Cottage Garden look, steer yourself away from placing everything symmetrically. This type of garden almost always looks a bit jumbled and that is part of its charm.

Making the cottage is either complex or simple, depending upon how far you take the design. You may choose to use as many or as few of the pattern elements as you please. You might want to have just the front of the cottage decorated and leave the sides and the back plain. Or you could skip doing the front peak and use the back wall and back part of the roof pattern in place of the front pieces (fig. 1).

CATMINT COTTAGE

Materials and Supplies

To be used in addition to the general Tools and Supplies list.

Fabrics:

- 1 yard for the roof – I used RJR™ Danscapes Architectural Wood Shingles in Dark Brown
- 1 yard for the siding (outer walls) – I used Elizabeth's Studio, Biffy – Crackle Wood Planks 1705.
- 1 yard for the lining (inside walls) – I wanted to use a sweet little surprise fabric for my lining and found a wonderful Spoonflower fabric called "Tiny Selvages."
- ½ yard for the white trim – I used Robert Kaufman Kona Cotton Solid in Bleach White K001-1287 PFD.
- ¼ yard for the doors and shutters – I used RJR Dan Morris Architectural Blue Wood 1424 06.
- ¼ yard for the window panes – I used Robert Kaufman Kona Cotton Solid in Light Parfait 1205.
- ¼ yard for the stonework and bricks – I used two fabrics, Avlyn® Fabrics Java Sketchbook Batik Builder Bricks Tan and South Seas Imports Patchwork Garden Stones.
- ½ to 1½ yards for the gardens or other design elements – It all depends on the scale, as well as how much of the print you can utilize. I used Timeless Treasures C9290, Green garden scene.
- 2 yards of Stiff Stuff Firm

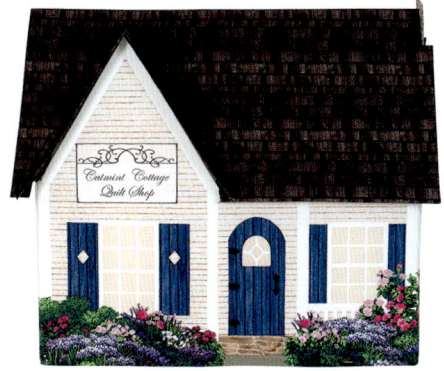

Fig. 1. View of all four sides of the cottage.

Lara Buccella · · · · · **Crafted Appliqué:** New Possibilities

Catmint Cottage

- 4 yards of Fusi-Bond Lite
- Fabri-tac Permanent Adhesive from Beacon Adhesives
- 77" of ⅝" sticky backed Velcro strips
- (1) 8½" x 11" sheet inkjet printable fabric
- Mod Podge – both the Fabric and gloss formulas
- Patterns

Instructions

Using the Patterns

First, refer to (pp. 12–13) for printing instructions. The patterns for the cottage are found on p. 92–94

You will need to make full size patterns for:
- One front cottage panel
- One back cottage panel
- Two side cottage panels
- The three roof sections
- The Chimney

The windows, shutters, doors, railings and trellis all will be cut from these same patterns after they have been used to create the walls. Be sure to leave them intact as you work.

Fabric preparation

Prewashing the fabrics will help the fusible web adhere better.

Fusible Web

Do not apply Mod Podge to the siding, lining, roof, or chimney fabrics. They will be adhered to the Stiff Stuff with fusible web interfacing. In this situation, fusible web provides the best bond.

Gloss Mod Podge

I suggest using Gloss Mod Podge to prepare the, railings, trellis, and window grille fabrics. Gloss Mod Podge creates a much stronger bond and that helps when working with very tiny pieces. But please be aware that, once it is adhered with high heat, the appliqué is there to stay. Any attempts at removal will ruin the appliqué and stretch the background fabric.

You can work around the super strong bond created with Gloss Mod Podge by first using the lowest setting on your iron and fusing by holding the iron in place for only 4 or 5 seconds. Repositioning appliqués becomes easy and it will not damage the fabrics to do so. Once you are sure you like what you see, then set your iron on the highest setting recommended for your fabric and iron the appliqués on permanently.

Fabric Mod Podge

For the remainder of the fabrics: the trim work, doors, and shutters Fabric Mod Podge is the most effective treatment.

Backcoating Light Fabrics

Use the backcoating technique on the windowpanes, white trim fabrics, and quilt shop sign. This is described in the section on Fabric Preparation (pp. 15–16). It makes a world of difference because it prevents the fabric behind these pieces from showing through.

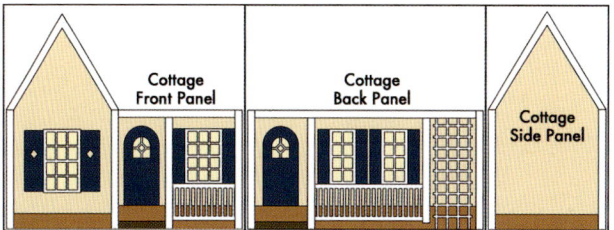

Fig. 2. Cottage Wall panel patterns

Building the Cottage

Wall Panels

Take a look at this sweet selvage dot fabric that I used for lining my cottage! It could just as well be the outside of one of these houses. I found it on Spoonflower.com in Christina Cameli's shop – afewscraps.

To get started with the construction of your cottage, you will need:

- Full size patterns for the front, back, and side panels of the cottage (fig. 2)
- The siding and lining fabrics, prewashed and pressed flat (fig. 3)
- Stiff Stuff sew-in interfacing
- Fusi-Bond Lite, or another fusible web interfacing

Fig. 3. Inside the lining of the front wall panel

Trim around the outside of the cottage panel patterns, leaving a small white margin around each (fig. 4). Set aside.

Apply fusible web to the wrong side of each piece of fabric. Let it cool completely and then peel off the backing paper in one whole piece. Set aside the backing paper to use as a pressing sheet later on.

Fig. 4. Placing the cottage front pattern over the fabric panel.

Iron the lining fabric to one side of the Stiff Stuff and then flip it over and iron the house siding fabric to the other side of the Stiff Stuff. Make sure that any directional prints in the

Catmint Cottage

Fig. 5. Cottage front fabric panel after it is cut out.

fabrics line up evenly with the straight edges of the Stiff Stuff and with each other.

Use transparent tape along the edges of the house pattern pieces to secure them to the front of each siding/Stiff Stuff/ lining sandwich (fig. 4). It is especially important to make sure that the print in your siding fabric runs parallel with the horizontal lines in the patterns. Cut out around the outline of each piece, using a ruler and rotary cutter or scissors (fig. 5).

Now you are ready to start adding the architectural features.

As you work, remember to protect your ironing board with either one of the saved fusible web backing sheets, freezer paper turned shiny side toward the sticky stuff, or a non-stick pressing sheet.

Foundation and Porch Floors

Next, cut out Mod Podge treated fabric strips for the porches and house foundation. The foundation strips are 1½" wide. The porch floor strips are 2" wide.

Use the front and back patterns as a guide for layout. Press the foundations and porch floors to the outside of the cottage panels, leaving a ½" overhanging the bottom. Iron and let cool. Then fold the overhanging portion of the strips over and around to the back of the panel. Iron and let cool. Cut out and add stairs to the porches if desired.

Windows & Grilles, Porch Posts, Railings, and Trellis

There are different ways you can create the windows and railings and I experimented until I found my favorite. A small, sharp pair of scissors for fine, detailed cutting is a must.

First, make the background windowpanes.

Carefully cut out each window, trim and all, from the main paper patterns along the outer edges of the entire window frame, leaving the surrounding pattern intact. Don't forget to cut out the little windows in the doors.

- Lay each window pattern onto the back of the windowpane fabric. Next, place a pressing sheet over them and fuse the patterns to the fabric with an iron. Let cool and then remove the pressing sheet. Finger pressing will not create a strong enough bond and you will need that as you do all the detailed snipping.

- Cut out the windows for the walls along the outside edges of the patterns. Then carefully peel the patterns off.

Cut out the windowpanes for the doors slightly larger than their patterns.

Next, use the same patterns to make the window frames and grilles. I found that I got the best result by hand cutting the frame work and white grilles as one whole piece and then laying it over a rectangle of the windowpane fabric. The same thing applied to cutting out the trellis and porch railings. Hand cutting was actually easier for me in the long run. It's not perfect, but it looks more charming.

- This time, iron the patterns onto the back of the white trim work fabric.

- Now cut the windowpanes out of each window, leaving the white trims and grilles as one whole piece. It works well to use the tip of your scissors to snip a small hole in the center of each windowpane and then work the scissors around, cutting in an ever widening circle, until you can safely cut out the rectangular windowpanes.

- Do the same for the porch railings and trellis, but extend the ends a little further past the patterns as shown with the dotted lines in (fig. 6). I have described an alternative method for making windows on (p. 46) in the chapter It's Super Quilter!

Once you have the components cut out, you are ready to work on putting them together.

- Place a pressing sheet shiny side up on your ironing board and lay the windows out on the sheet, right sides up. Very carefully lay each window grille over its corresponding window. Make sure that the grilles are not stretched or distorted and that the Modge Podged sides are facing down.

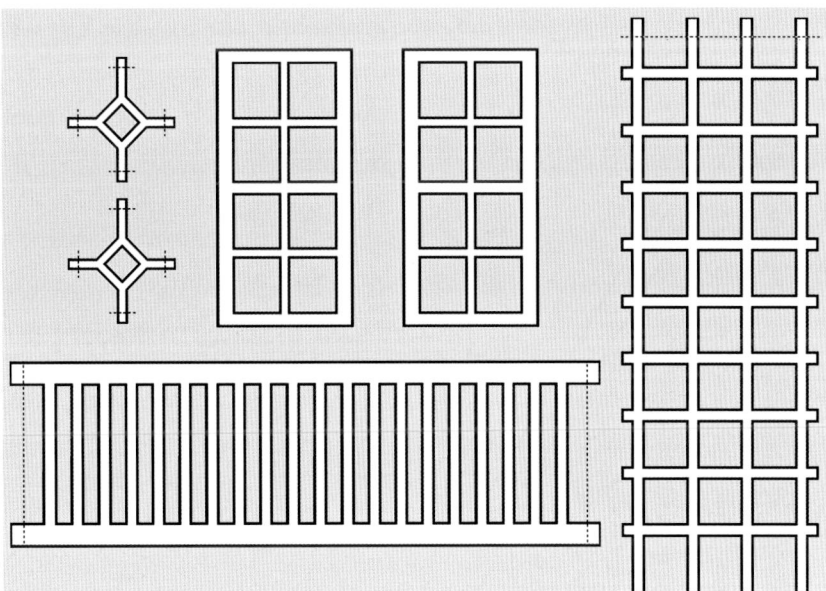

Fig. 6. Diagram showing window grills, railing and trellis cut outs

Catmint Cottage

Place a pressing sheet over your work and fuse the appliqués together.

- Lay the completed windows on the wall panels, using the original pattern to place position them (set aside the door windows until later). Fuse in place.
- Follow the same procedure for the railings and trellis, only lay those directly onto the wall panels, using the original panel pattern as a placement guide.

Porch Columns

Next, cut ½" wide strips for the porch columns. Position them on the wall panel as shown in the pattern and then fuse them in place.

Top Trim

Cut 1⅛" wide strips for the top trim pieces. Use your pattern to cut each piece to the right length. Fold each strip in half, lengthwise, and finger crease it down the middle.

Lay the trim strips along the top edges and peaks of each wall panel. Place the crease you made on the ridge, with ½" draping over the front and ½" left to wrap around the backside.

Press the strips in place on the front of each wall panel. Now flip the panel over. Fold the trim piece around to the back of the panel, and press in place.

When you do the strips at the top of the peaks, create mitered corners by laying one strip on whole and folding it around to the back. Then lay the second strip over that and cut the strip in an angle. Refer to (fig. 7). The dotted line shows how the trim piece should be cut.

Doors and Shutters

Cut the doors and shutters from the main paper patterns. Fuse them to the back of their fabric and cut out the appliqués. Let cool and then peel off the paper. Fuse the windows to the back of the doors. Position the appliqués on the wall panels as in the original pattern and iron them in place.

The Chimney – Part 1

Print the chimney pattern (p. 94) to scale. Roughly cut out the pattern, leaving a small margin all the way around.

- Apply fusible web to the wrong side of the chimney fabric. Use the pattern to cut out the fabric.

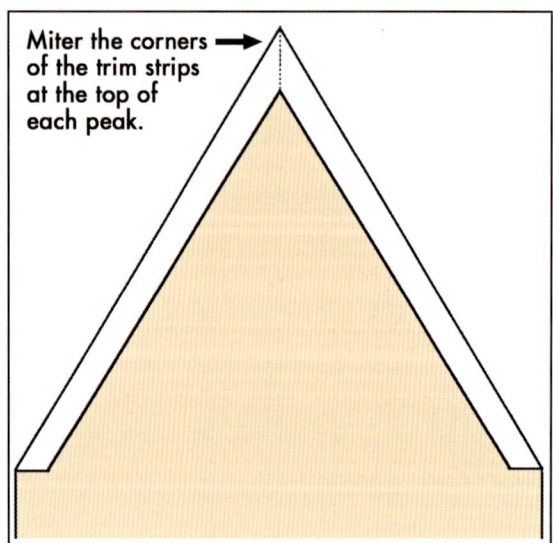

Fig. 7. Cutting the mitered angle from the trim at the peak

- Now lay the pattern over a piece of Stiff Stuff, tape it around the edges, and cut out the Stiff Stuff panel in the center.

- Lay the Stiff Stuff panel on the wrong side of the fabric, being careful to orient the fabric design in the right direction, and fuse the fabric to the panel.

- Trim and fold the fabric around to the back. Fuse in place.

Cottage Shop Sign and Barn Quilts

Scan the shop sign patterns into your computer (p.82). You can create your own sign in a photo or paint program. You can also make your own barn quilts this way, or with quilting software, such as EQ®. Print the sign and barn quilts onto an inkjet fabric sheet.

Prepare the back of the fabric sheet with Fabric Mod Podge. Backcoat the quilt shop sign to ensure that it will not be translucent. Let dry.

Cut out the sign and quilts. Fuse and then stitch them to the cottage panels and chimney.

The Chimney – Part 2

Cut out a piece of fusible web the size of the chimney and apply it to the back of the chimney, making sure not to go higher than the future roofline. Let cool and peel off the paper backing.

Place the chimney in position on its side wall panel. Fuse in place.

Sew the chimney to the wall panel, quilting along the edges of the bricks or stones and around the border of the barn quilt.

Corners

Cut 1⅛" wide strips for the corner trim pieces. Use your pattern to cut each piece to the right length. Fold each strip in half and finger crease it down the middle.

Lay the trim strips along the side edges of the front and back wall panels. The side wall panels will not have corner strips until all the panels are joined together. Place the crease just off the edge, with the other half left free. Fig. 8 shows all the architectural elements on the back wall panel. The dotted lines on the right and left indicate where the corner strips overlap the edges of the panel.

Press the strips in place on the front surface of each wall panel. Let cool and then peel the panel off the pressing sheet.

Fig. 8. Cottage back wall panel with all the appliqués and corner trim

CATMINT COTTAGE

Planting the Garden

Prepare your embellishment fabrics with Gloss Mod Podge. It creates a stronger bond, so you don't have to stress out about sewing every little detail and can simply sew the appliqués on in a way that looks best.

Simply cut out the plants and flowers from the prepared fabrics and place them in pleasing arrangements along the bottoms of the wall panels.

For the front and back elevations, create extensions of the gardens so that they will blend nicely with the gardens around the corner. For the side elevations, stop placing plants once you reach the area where the corner trim piece will go (fig. 9).

Lightly fuse all the plants in place, with your iron set on its lowest heat setting. Prop the wall panels up vertically and step back and take a look at your work. When you are happy with each arrangement, fuse the appliqués on permanently with the iron set on high.

Stitching the Appliqués

Use matching thread whenever possible on all the architectural elements. For most of the gardens around CATMINT COTTAGE, I used YLI invisible thread in smoke. For the light pink and white plants, I switched to YLI in clear.

I have a little trick I use when I sew over the light colored appliqués but don't like the appearance of the needle holes. After I remove the piece from the sewing machine, I go over those areas using a very fine needle

Fig. 9. Extending the front to garden past the edges

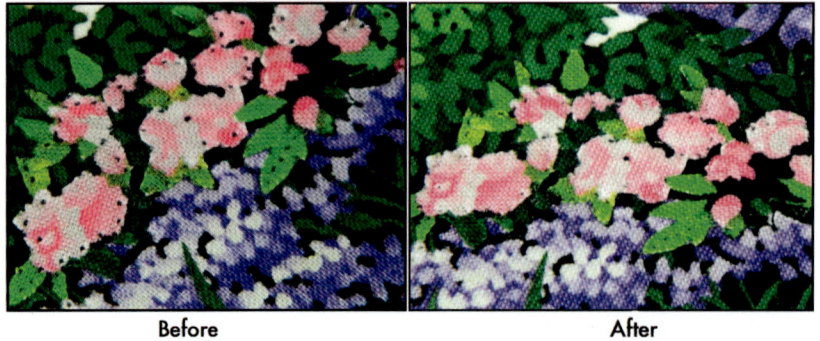

Fig. 10. Needle holes: now you see them, now you don't

to push the fabric's thread closer around the machine needle holes (fig. 10).

There are ways to make the stitching look more natural as you go along, as well as hold the appliqués down nicely. Here are a few tips:

- Don't sew right across the lighter colored plants. Even with clear invisible thread, this can look messy.

- Head the stitching down the center of tiny leaves and don't worry about the edges. When you get to the tip of a leaf or a finely cut point, make sure to take one more stitch off the point of the appliqué into the background fabric. This way, the tip won't bend up.

- For very fine, thin pieces, don't sew right through them because they might end up pushed out of position or even broken. Instead, do a small serpentine stitch with invisible thread, zigzagging back and forth over the piece to hold it down.

- I do a hand turned wiggle stitch, when sewing along the edges of tiny floral appliqués (fig. 11). I wiggle the piece back and forth as I go along. I use this when I need to create a more natural look with an outline that is not so sharply delineated.

You might wonder how to do a zigzag or wiggle stitch if your sewing machine only has a straight stitch (fig. 12). I do it on my machine by decreasing the presser foot pressure just a little bit, which allows for some wiggle room without lifting the foot.

Keep in mind that anything you outline with your stitching will be pulled in tighter to the panel. It will look like it is recessed back behind the surrounding fabrics. The window grilles are an example of this. I opted to stitch only around the outside of each window to hold it all in place. I found that trying to stitch those tiny grilles distorted them and made them look too pushed in, so I left them plain. There is no worry that they will fray, so this is fine to do.

Fig. 11. Close up of the flowers and bird bath sewn in place

Fig. 12. Close up of a hand turned wiggle stitch

CATMINT COTTAGE

Fig. 13. Shows how to stitch the corners in place

Fig. 14. Cottage panels, front and right side joined

Fig. 15. Cottage panels, back and left side joined

Sewing the panels together

- Once you have the appliqués sewn onto each of the four wall panels, it is time to join the walls together.

- Cut four inside corner strips of trim fabric, 7¾" long x 1½" wide. Iron fusible web to their backs.

- Work with two panels at a time. Line them up in the correct order on your ironing board, right sides up, and scoot them close to each other, leaving a 1/16" gap between the panels. That gap is important, so do not accidently readjust it. The corner trims and garden plants on the front or back wall panels should perfectly overlap the side panel. Iron the corner trim and garden plants in place. Let cool.

- Turn each 2-panel unit over to the lining side. Lay the inside corner strip in place and fuse.

- Using matching thread, sew each corner on with four lines of stitching, an inner and outer line of stitches along each side. In Figure 13, the dotted lines show where the four lines of stitching should be.

- Before changing your thread, sew the corner together on the second 2-panel unit.

- Switch back to invisible thread and appliqué the corner plantings.

- Next, lay out the two 2-panel units in the correct order and repeat the previous steps.

- Lastly, join the 4th and last corner

·76· Crafted Appliqué: New Possibilities · · · · · Lara Buccella together with this same procedure. You will be working inside the boxed walls this time, but the Stiff Stuff is flexible enough that it is not overly difficult to iron and sew on the pieces.

It's Time to Build the Roof
Creating the Roof Panels

To get started with the construction of the roof, you will need:

- Full size patterns for Main Roof Panels 1 and 2 and Secondary Roof Panels 3 and 4.
- The roof fabric, prewashed and pressed flat.
- Stiff Stuff Sew-In interfacing.
- Fusi-Bond Lite, or another fusible web interfacing.

Apply fusible web to the wrong side of the roof fabric. Set aside.

Cut out the roof panel patterns. Place the patterns on the Stiff Stuff. Use clear scotch tape along the edges to hold them in place and cut them out.

Lay the fusible web backed fabric on your ironing board, wrong side up. Flip the Stiff Stuff panels over, so that they are a mirror image of the patterns. Place the panels on the fabric in sets of two: Panels 1 and 2 will form the Main Roof (A) and Panels 3 and 4 will form the Secondary Roof (B). Move the paired panels together until they are 1/16" apart. Make sure that the fabric print runs parallel with the panel edges. Use masking tape to tape the pairs in place on the fabric.

Trim around each pair of panels, roughly 1/2" from the edges. Flip the panels over and fuse the fabric to the Stiff Stuff panels. Let cool.

Move the panels to your cutting board and trim the excess fabric off, right along the edge of the Stiff Stuff. This side of the panel sets will become the interior of the cottage roof. Remove the masking tape.

Lay the remainder of the fusible web backed roof fabric on your ironing board, wrong side up. This fabric will cover the exterior of the cottage roof. Place Roof A and Roof B on the fabric, Stiff Stuff sides down. Make sure that the fabric print runs parallel with the pattern edges. Fuse the outside roof fabric to the Stiff Stuff panels. Let cool.

Trim away the excess exterior fabric, leaving 1" flaps around the edges of Roof A and Roof B. Fig. 16, p. 78, shows the two roofs flipped so that the Exterior side of the panels is facing down.

Trim the flaps as shown in the diagram, but be careful never to snip the flaps closer than 1/8" away from the panel edge. You will need this little bit to cover the edge of the Stiff Stuff when you fold the flaps around the edges of the panels.

Wrap each flap around to the interior side of the roof panels and fuse in place. Be careful around the corners not to leave any raw edges or Stiff Stuff peeking out. On areas where the tabs overlap and do not have fusible web, use a small dab of fabric glue to hold them in place.

Catmint Cottage

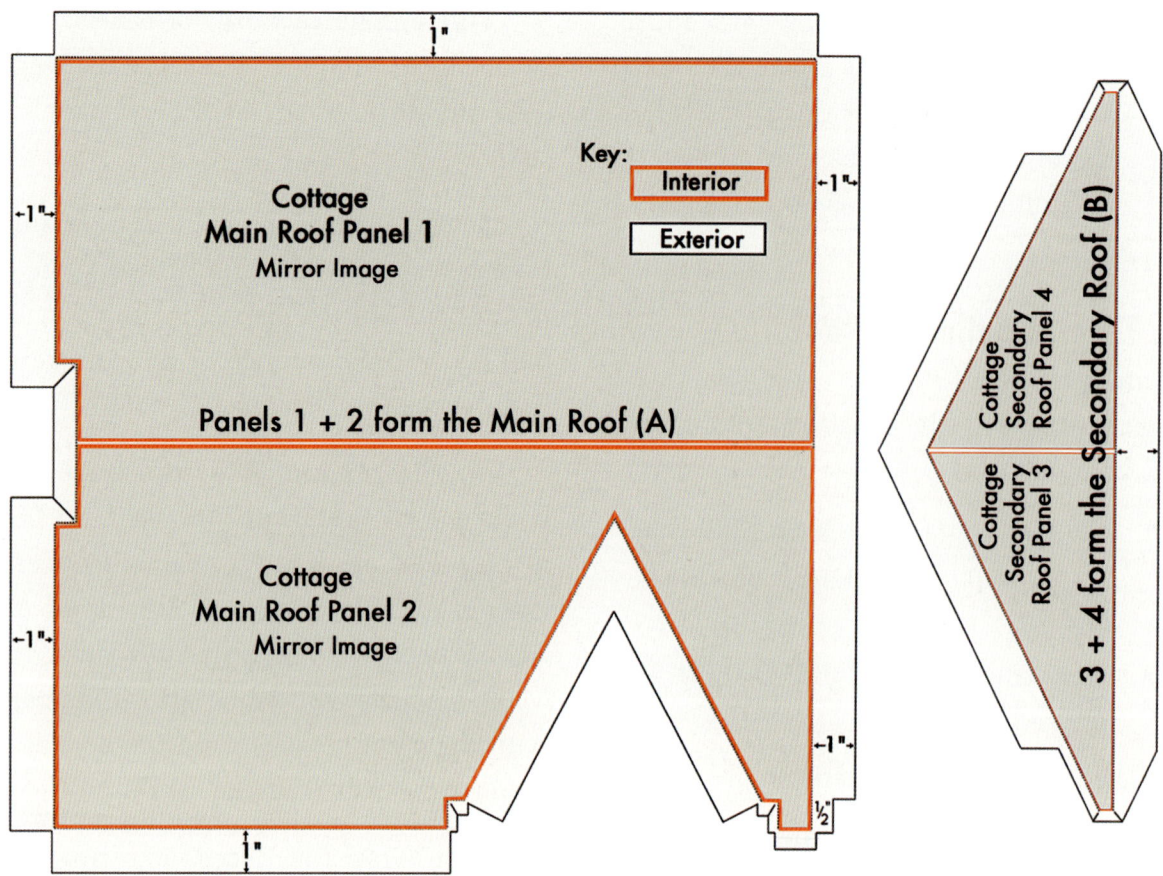

Fig. 16. Creating the roof panels

Fiddling with the Roof

Now that Roof A and Roof B are completely covered, it is time to sew. Add a double line of stitches along the 1/16" gap between Stiff Stuff panels on each roof. Next, stitch around the edges of the roofs. Sew quilted details as desired to help give the roof texture. I simply followed along the lines of shingles. Iron each panel and let cool.

Attaching the Roof to the Walls

The cottage walls and roof need to be held together, yet be easy to reposition. The best way I found to do this was to use Velcro tabs along the top of the walls and under the eaves of the roof.

Applying Velcro Tabs to the Walls

Apply fusible web interfacing to the back of the treated white fabric that you have left over from the trim pieces. Cut the fabric into 1½" wide strips.

Cut the strips in lengths that will fit along the top off the cottage walls and peaks. Crease the strips in half with the sticky side out. These will form the tabs that hold the Velcro up along the top of the walls.

Lay each tab sticky side down along the top inside of each wall panel. Leave half of the tab hanging over the wall. Protect your ironing board with a non-stick pressing sheet and fuse the tab in place.

When working with the tabs behind the chimney, you will also need to protect the chimney with a pressing sheet. I used a piece of the fusible web's paper backing and laid it shiny side up over the chimney and along the point of the roof. Then I fused the tabs in place.

Apply the loopy halves of the Velcro strips to the sticky side of the tabs, so that they stick out above the top of the walls. They should be facing out (fig. 17).

To apply Velcro strips to the inside of the roof:

Lay out Roof A and B. wrong sides up. Mark ¾" all around the straight edges of the roof panels. Do not do this on the angled edges of either panel.

Glue the "hook" half of the Velcro strips on, just inside the ¾" lines. Trim as shown (fig. 18).

Next, you will need to make another set of tabs to adhere Roof B to Roof A. These tabs will not have Velcro, but will be glued on. I highly recommend using Fabri-Tac Permanent Adhesive. It has a strong grip and sets up quickly.

To create the tabs, use Mod Podged fabric that matches the roof.

Cut two strips, ½" wide by 7⅞" long. Fold the strips lengthwise, Mod Podged side out and finger crease them down the middle.

Lay out Roof B with the Interior facing up.

Lay out the tabs, Mod Podged side facing up and apply a thin line of glue along one side of each crease.

Lay the tabs, glued line down, along the angled edges of Roof B, placing each tab halfway on and off the edge, so that the side with no glue sticks out past the edge.

Be very careful not to get glue on the Exterior surface of the roof. Let dry.

Fig. 17. Cottage walls showing the top lined along the inside with velcro tabs

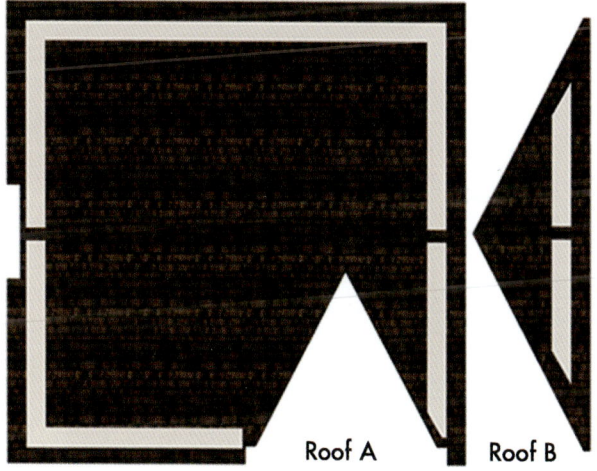

Fig. 18. Apply Velcro along the edges of Roof B and A.

Catmint Cottage

Fig. 19. Chalk in the position of Roof B

Fig. 20. Use masking tape to mark the outline

Fig. 21. Trim the tabs around the notches

Assembling the Roof

Place Roof A on the cottage walls, holding it in place with the Velcro tab and straight pins, if need be.

Position Roof B, so that it lies snugly against the roof pitch and so that the front peak of the cottage nestles into the roof with a ½" overhang. Mark the outline of Roof B on Roof A, **with** chalk (fig. 19).

Remove both Roof A and B from the Cottage.

Lay Roof A flat on the ironing board, with the Exterior facing up. Apply strips of masking tape along the outside of the chalk lines (fig. 20).

Lay Roof B in place and trim the inside tabs so they do not obstruct the notches on Roof A. (See fig. 21. The notches are indicated with arrows.)

Remove Roof B and flip it over so the tab side is facing up. Fold the tab down toward the interior of Roof B. Apply a thin line of glue along the outside of the crease, a little bit away from the roof edge (fig. 22).

Immediately place Roof B in its correct position on Roof A, inside the masking tape outline (fig. 23). Press all the edges together with your fingers. Be very careful not to squeeze the glue out past the edges onto the Exterior surface of either roof.

Hold the roof firmly in place, until the glue has a chance to set up. When the glue has a strong grip, remove the masking tape and let the glue dry the rest of the way.

Topping Off the Cottage

Once the glue is dry, the roof is ready to be placed on top of the cottage. Before you start, place masking tape over the fuzzy loop side of the Velcro tabs. This way you can remove the tape and attach one section of the walls at a time to the hook side of the Velcro on the roof, without all the others tabs grabbing hold all at once. Otherwise it will be like wrestling an octopus.

It takes a little bit of adjusting back and forth but it holds very well once you have everything in place. Don't forget to sign the inside of your cottage. You should be very proud of what you have accomplished!

Fig. 22. Apply glue to the outside of the folded tab

Fig. 23. Place Roof B inside the masking tape outlines

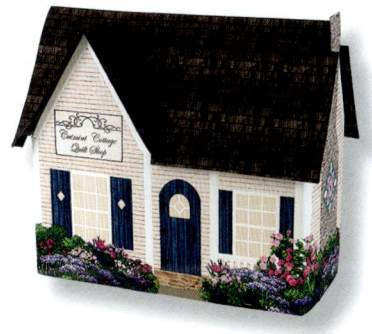

Designer Spotlight:
Christina Cameli

Tiny Selvage was created by Christina: author, teacher, blogger, Craftsy Instructor and designer. Christina wrote:

"Since I am not a professional fabric designer I have the freedom to design fabric solely for my pleasure. This print came about after I had pieced together a bunch of selvages into one piece of fabric. I loved the look of them all sewn together and wanted to be able to get that look without needing to sew it myself. I pulled out my selvage stash for reference and then stayed awake late into the night getting it just the way I wanted it. It's been fun to discover that other people are as delighted with the fabric as I am!"

Christina has a wonderful blog that you might like to check out:

A Few Scraps – www.afewscraps.com

Patterns

Catmint Cottage signs:
for inkjet printing on fabric
Shown at
100%

Catmint Cottage
©2016 Lara Buccella

Size check
this box
measures
1" x 1"

Enlarge Pattern
200%

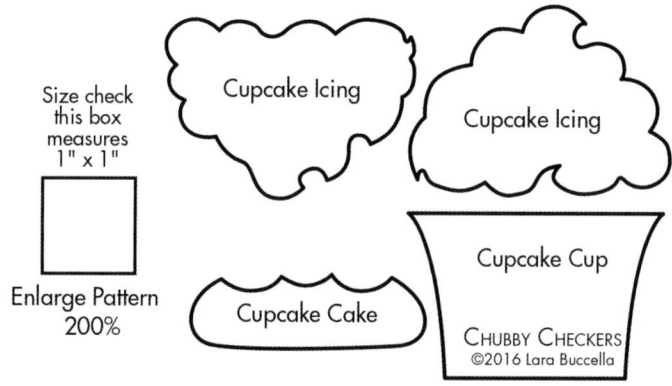

Cupcake Icing

Cupcake Icing

Cupcake Cake

Cupcake Cup

Chubby Checkers
©2016 Lara Buccella

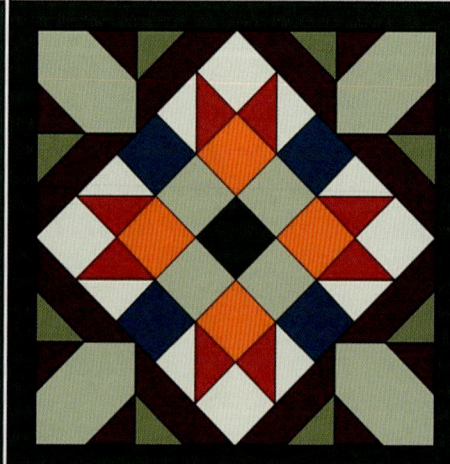

Crafted Appliqué: New Possibilities · · · · Lara Buccella

The Walking Tree

Pattern and layout diagram

Walking Tree
©2016 Lara Buccella

size check
this box
measures 1"

Enlarge pattern
365%

Cecropia Utopia

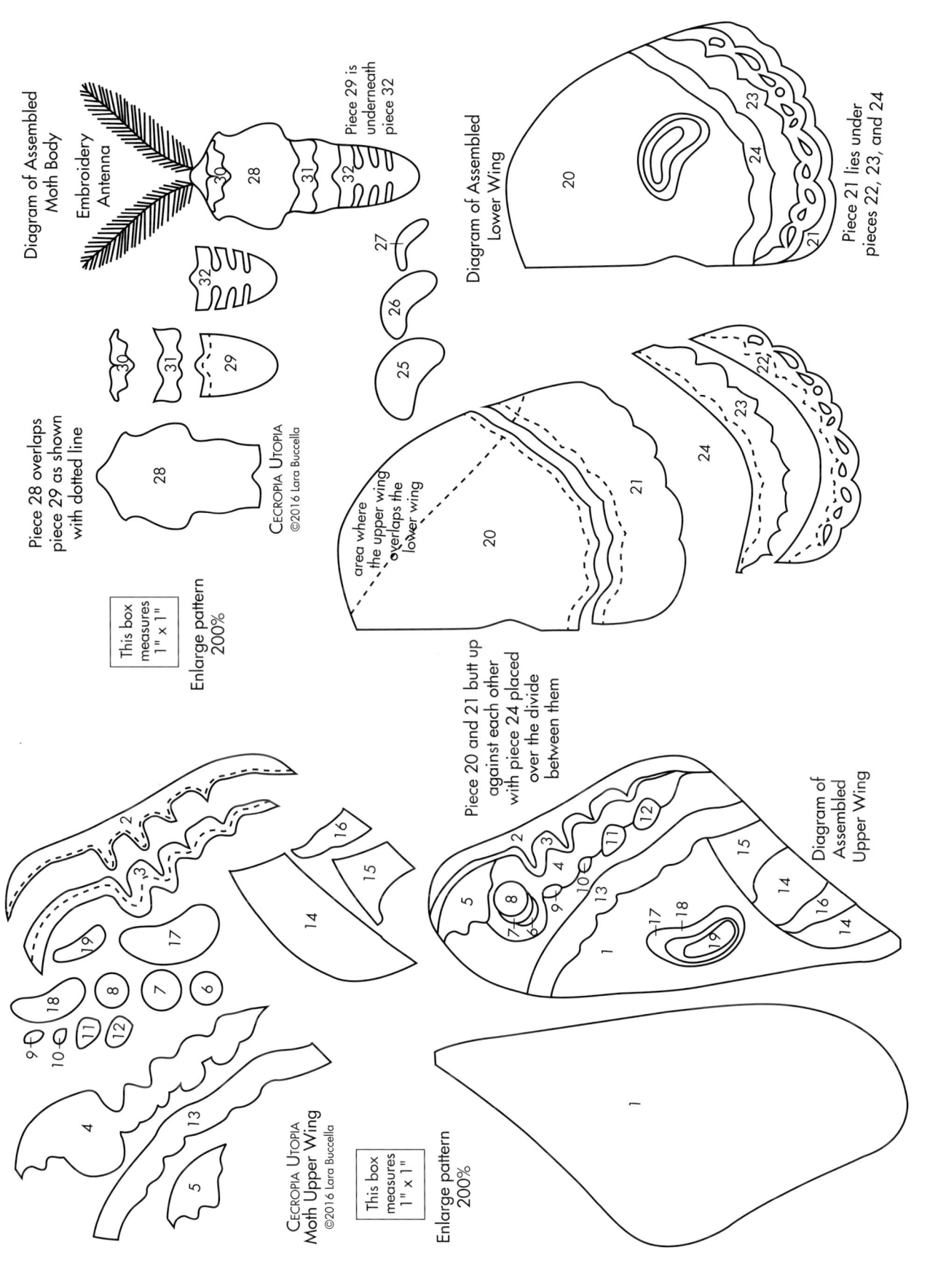

It's Super Quilter

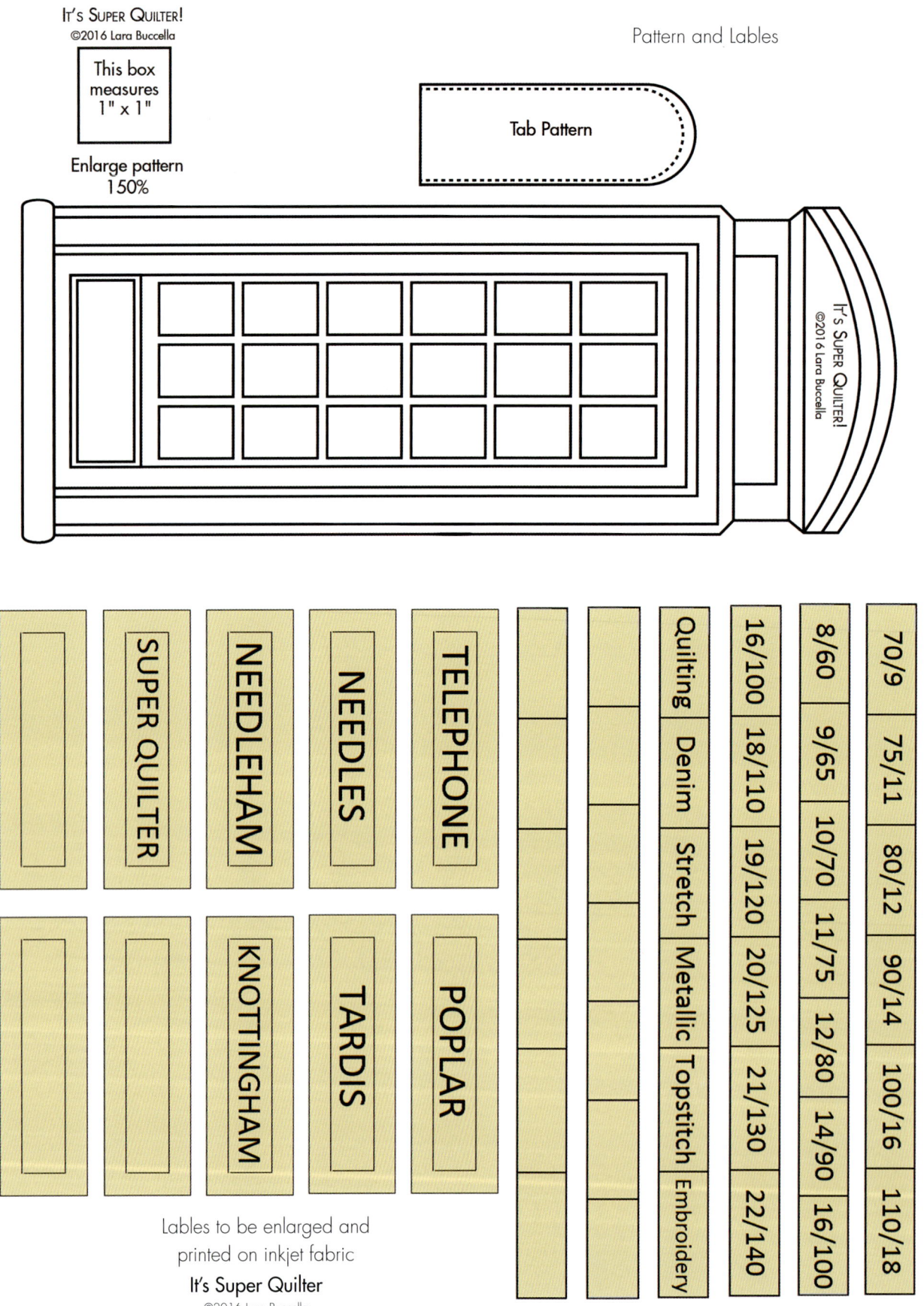

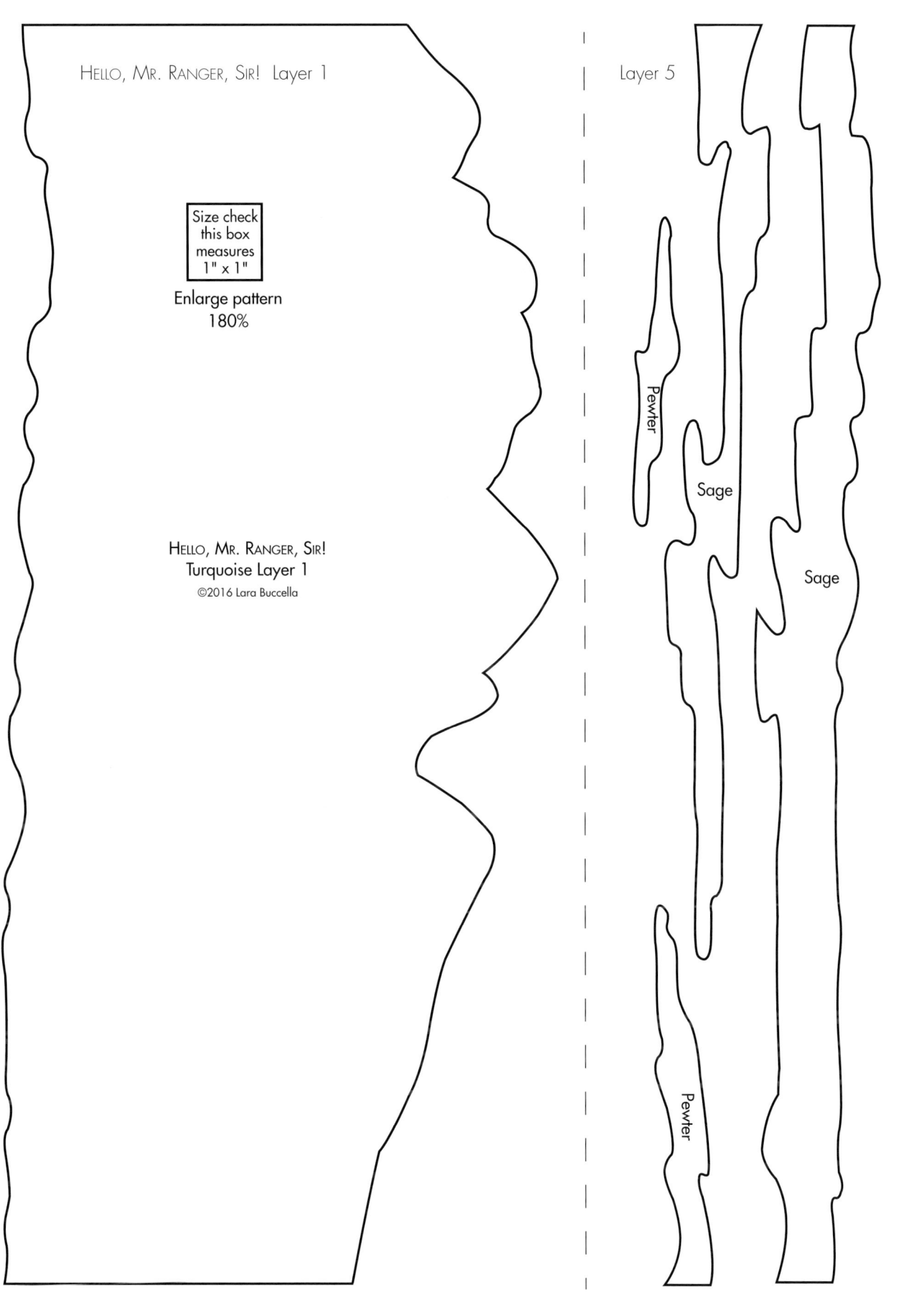

Hello Mr. Ranger, Sir!

Hello, Mr. Ranger, Sir! Layer 2

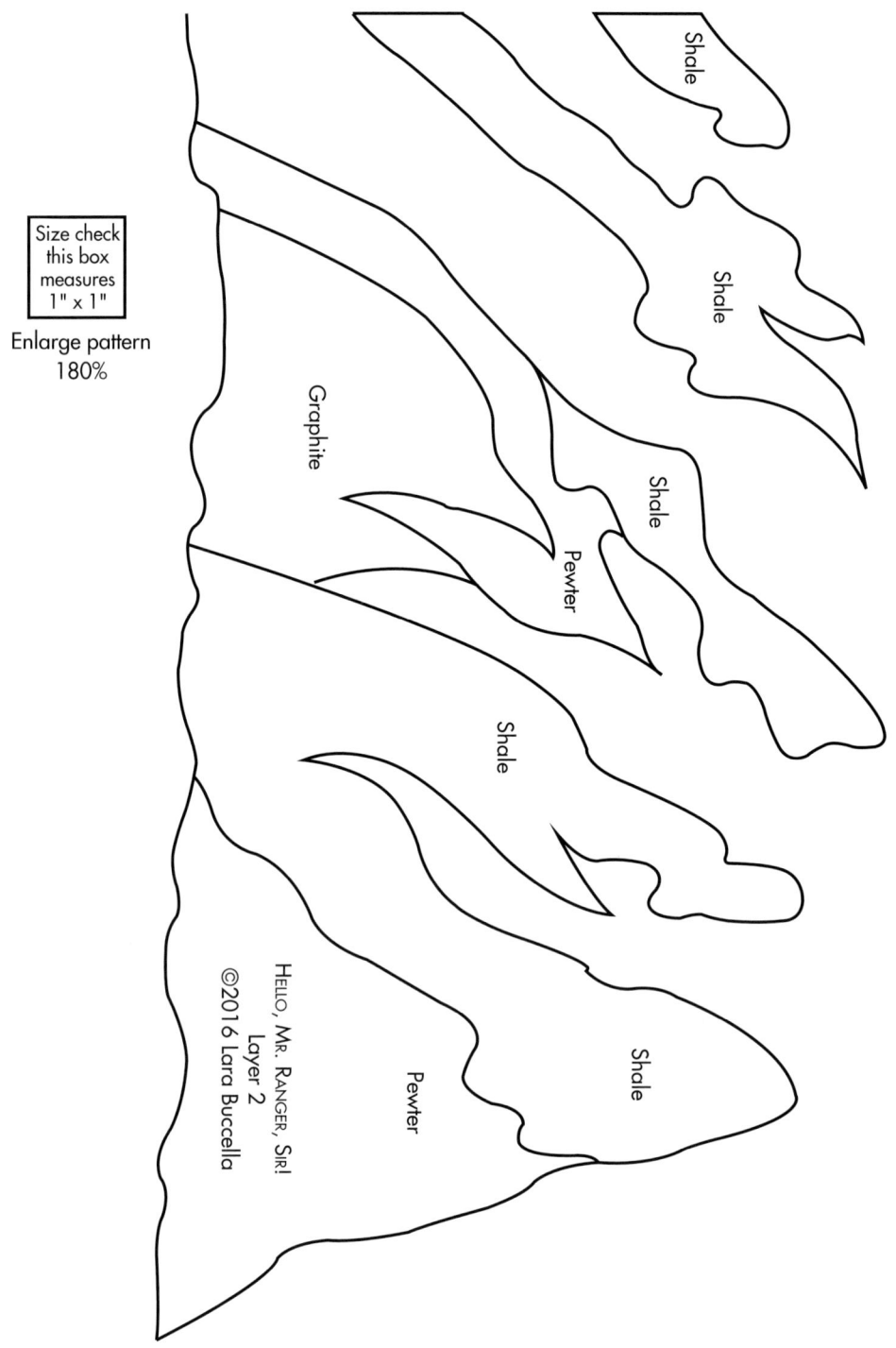

HELLO MR. RANGER, SIR!

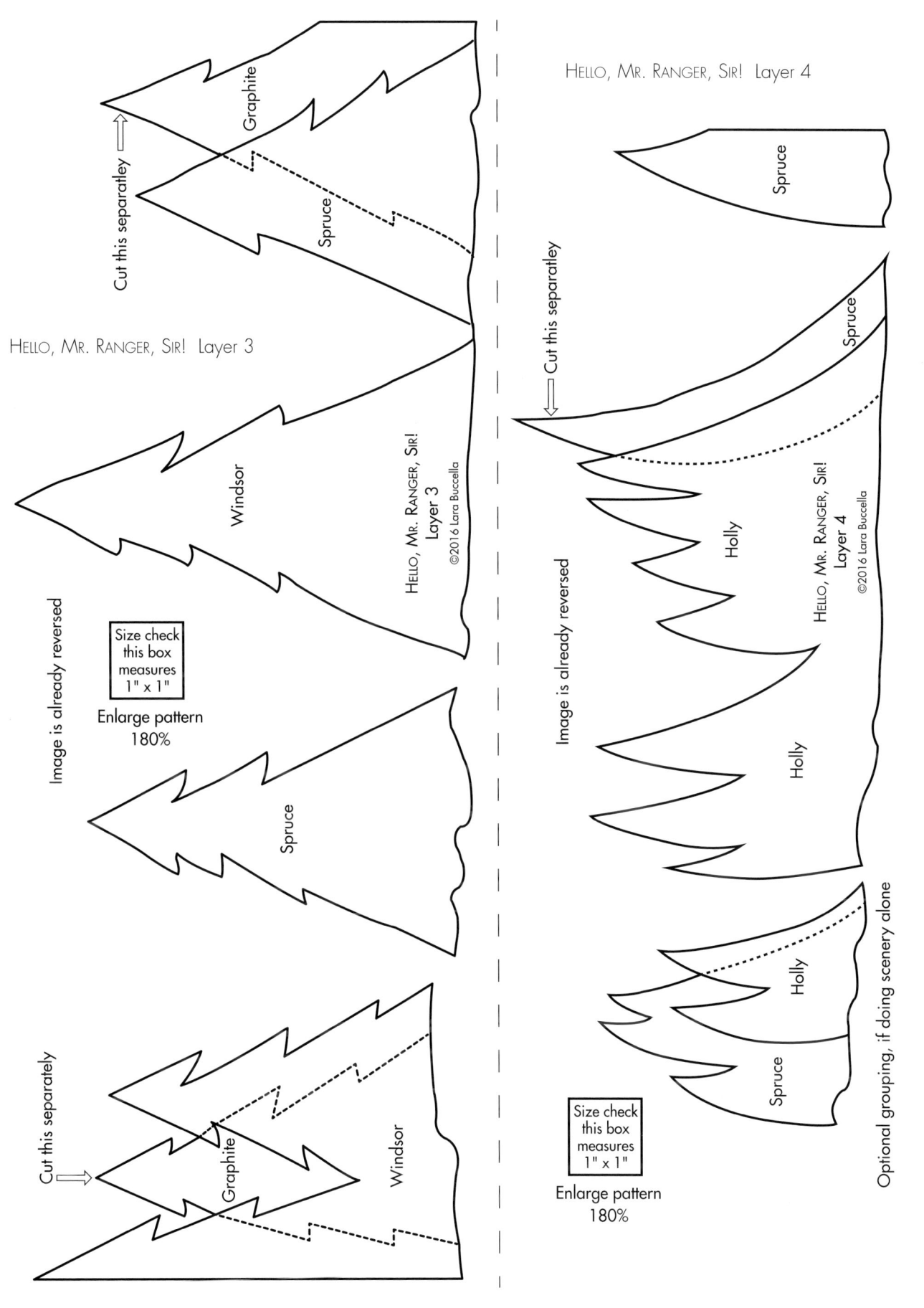

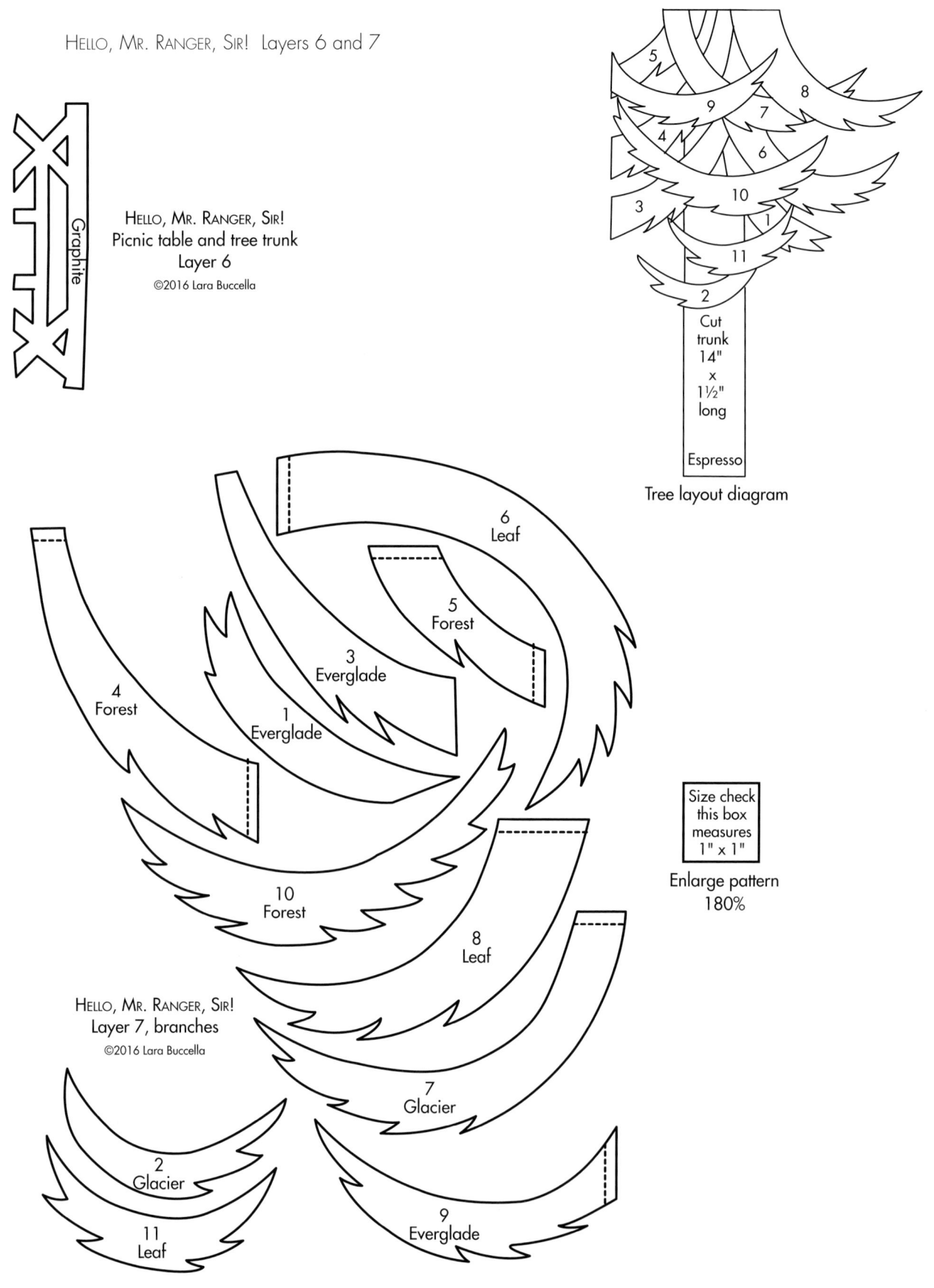

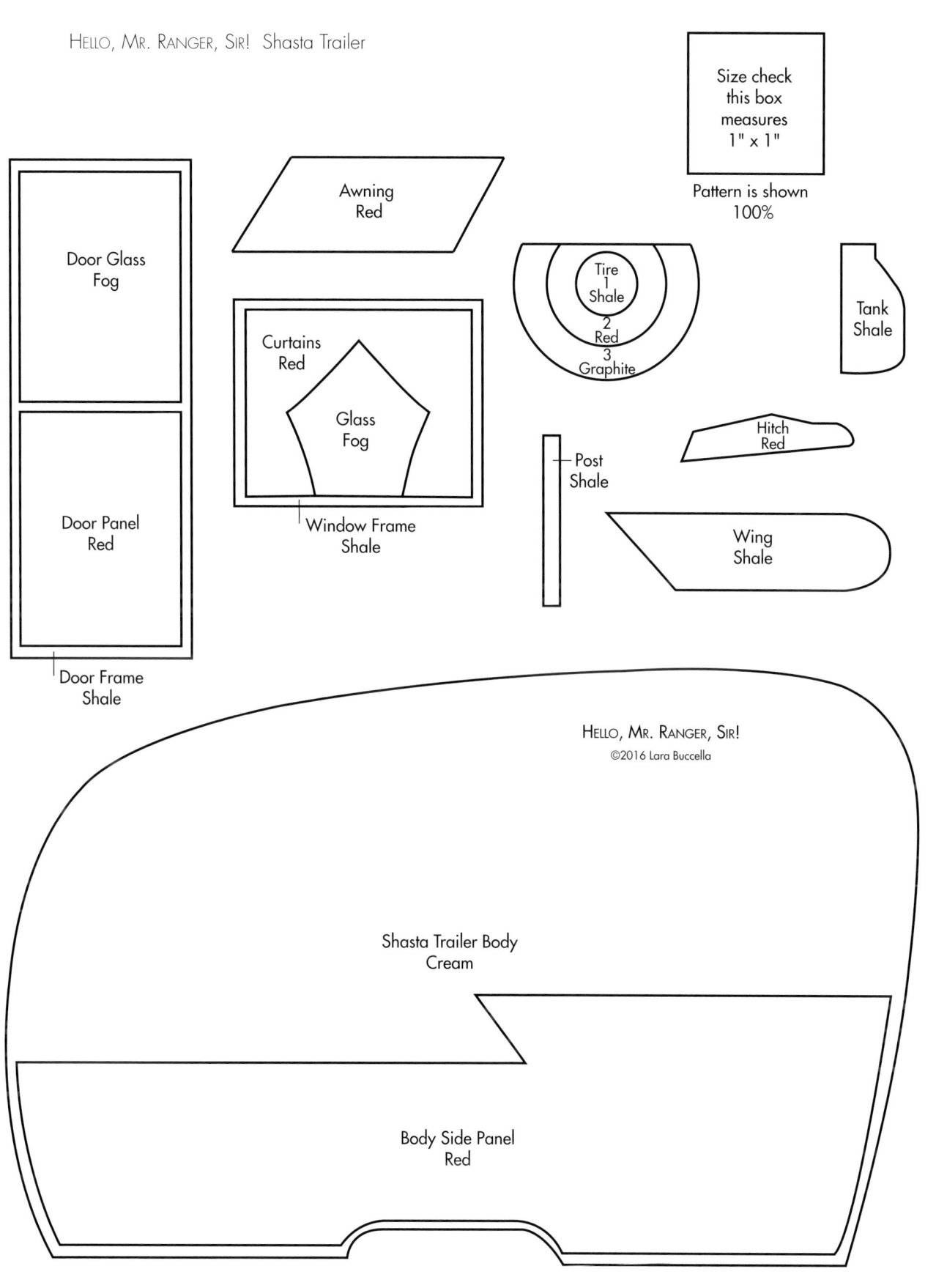

Catmint Cottage

· 92 · Crafted Appliqué: New Possibilities · · · · · Lara Buccella

Catmint Cottage

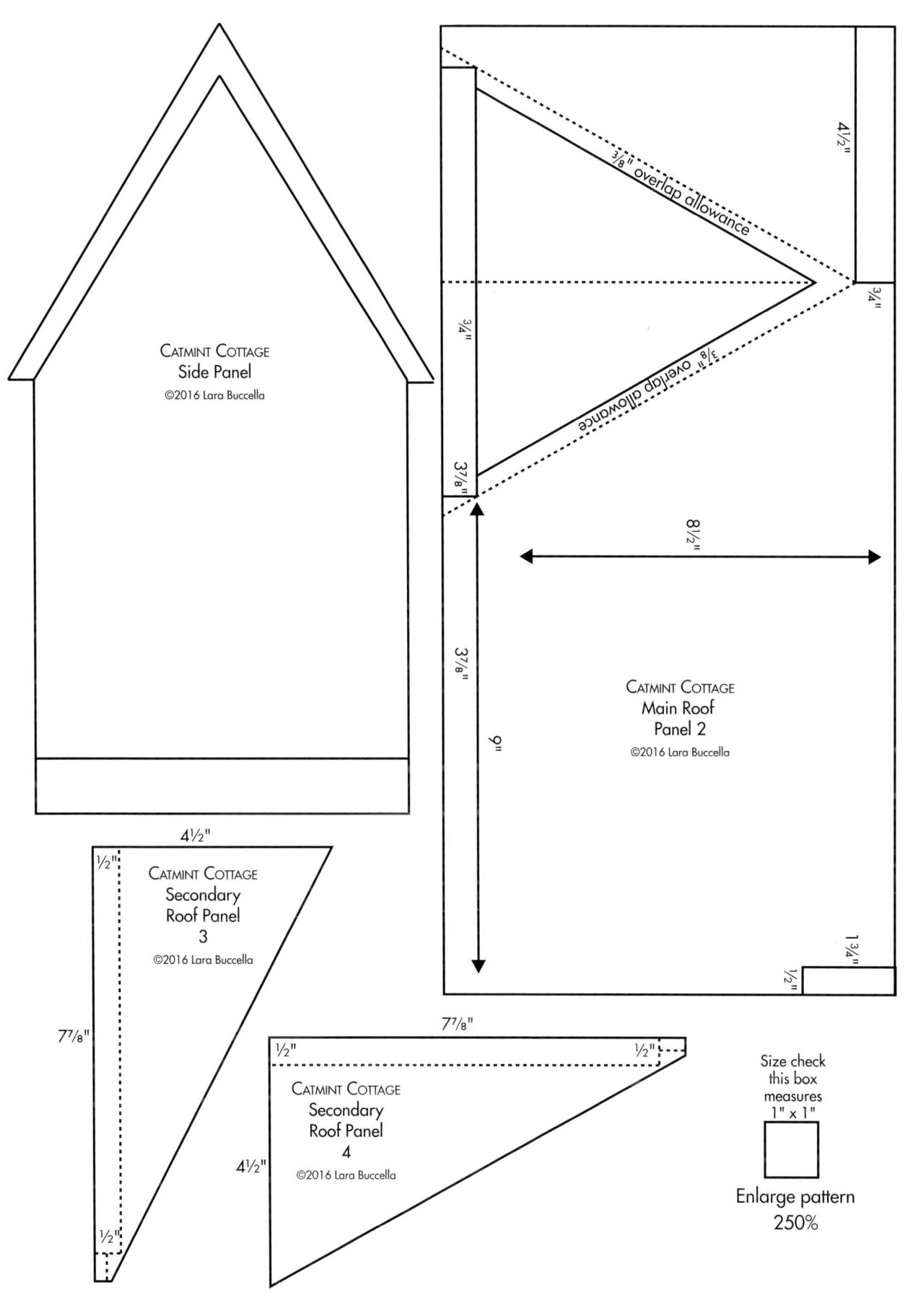

Lara Buccella · · · · **Crafted Appliqué:** New Possibilities

Catmint Cottage

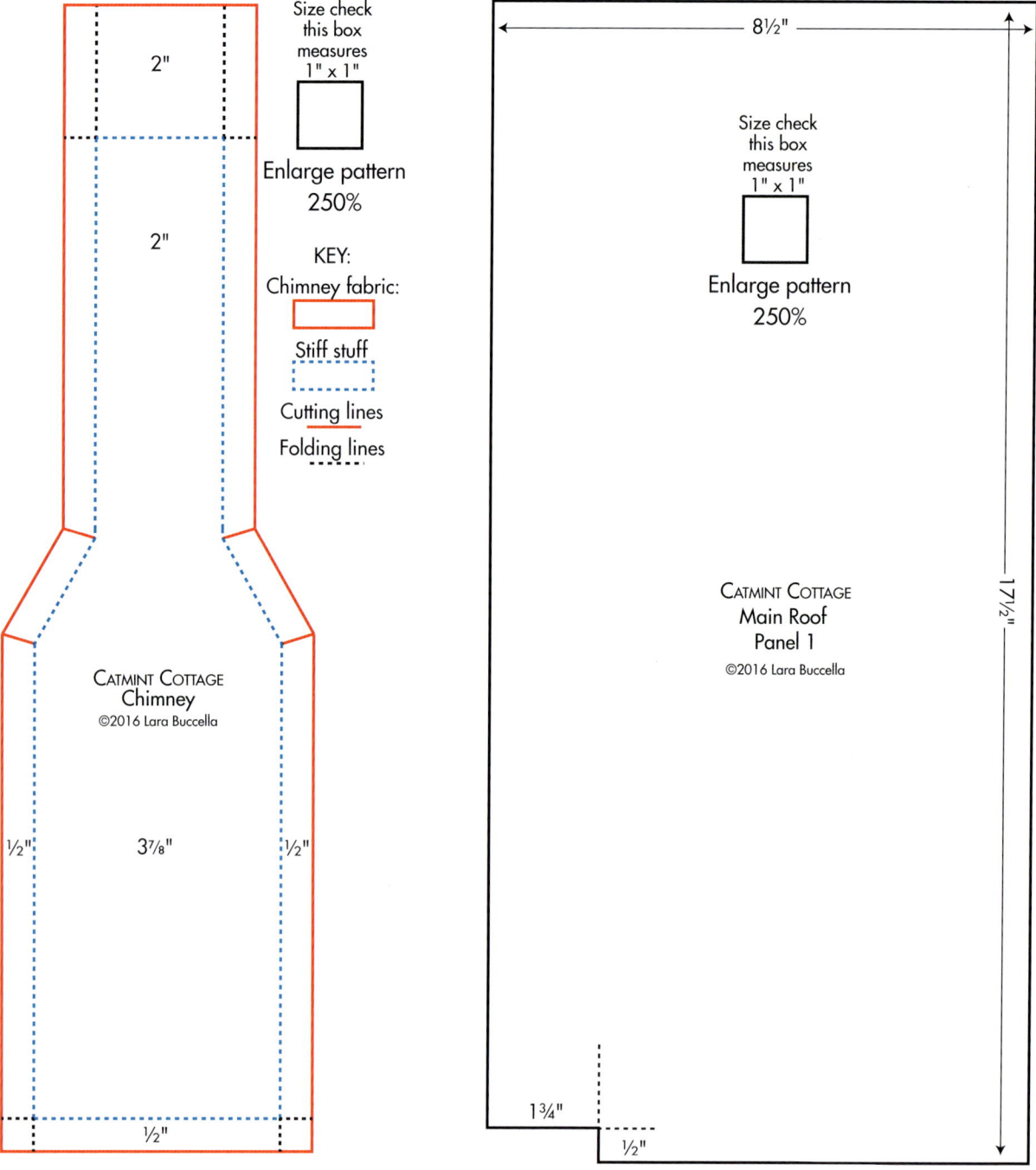

Resources

Stiff Stuff Interfacing:
http://www.lazygirldesigns.com/products/stiff-stuff

Fusi-Bond Lite:
http://www.lazygirldesigns.com/products/fusi-bond-lite

Plain Jane Threads: Oakshott Cottons
plainjanethreads.com

Erica's Craft and Sewing Center: Interfacings from Lazy Girl Designs
http://www.ericas.com/sewing/lazygirlinterfacing.htm

The Fat Quarter Shop: Kona cotton solid fabrics
http://www.fatquartershop.com/

Fabrics from Independent designers:
http://www.spoonflower.com/

About the Author

Photo by: Nicole M. Stuart

Lara Buccella lives in western New York with her husband Jim and their two terriers. She is the mother of three wonderful young people, mother-in-law to a terrific young man, and a brand new grandmother.

A lifelong love of arts and crafts led Lara to take up quilting after her youngest child left for college. Even before completing her first quilt, a One Block Wonder, she realized that she had found her creative voice. With more than forty years of sewing and fabric petting **experience**, becoming a quilter was a natural fit.

Over the years, Lara has taught many different kinds of crafts to groups of all ages. Always one to play around with and mix techniques, she often sets off on her own path. This has led to some interesting adventures in quilting. You can take a peek at what she's up to by visiting her blog at www.buzzinbumble.com.

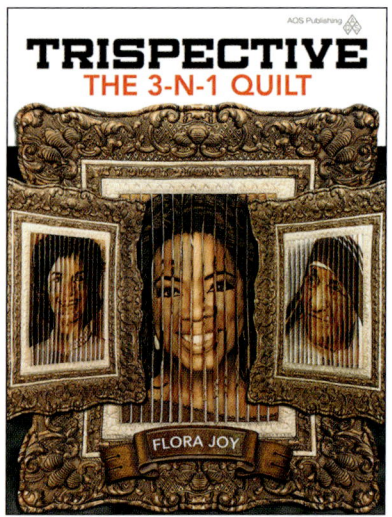
#10281

#10279

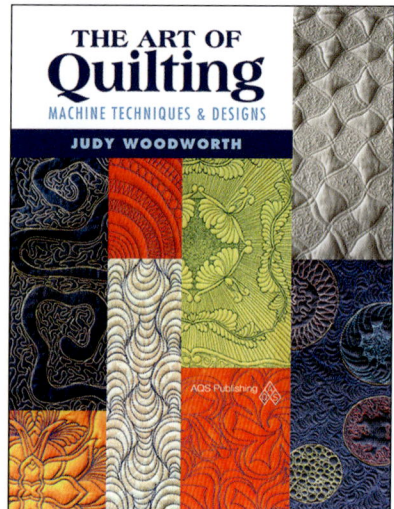
#11140

Enjoy these and more from AQS

AQS Publishing brings the latest in quilt topics to satisfy the traditional to modern quilter. Interesting techniques, vivid color, and clear directions make these books your one-stop for quilt design and instruction. With its leading Quilt-Fiction series, mystery, relationship, and community all merge as stories are pieced together to keep you spell-bound.

Whether Quilt-Instruction or Quilt-Fiction, pick one up from AQS today.

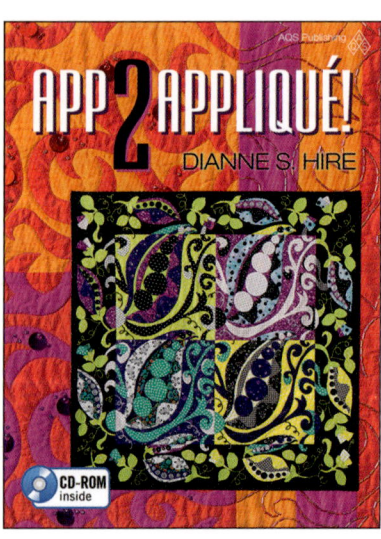
#10280

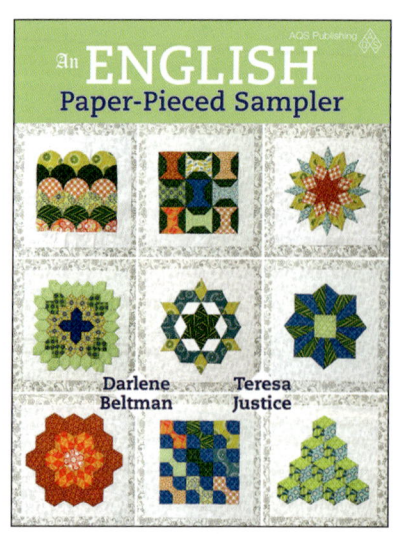
#10272

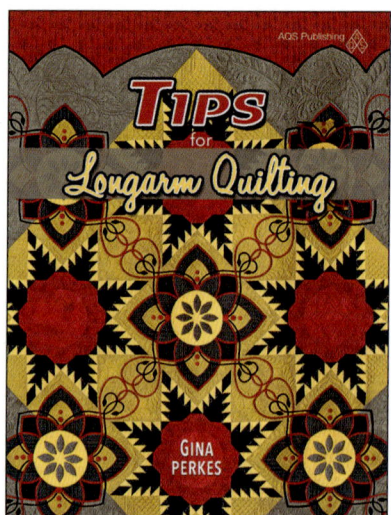
#10285

Crafted Appliqué
New Possibilities
· Lara Buccella ·

American Quilter's Society
www.AmericanQuilter.com

The American Quilter's Society or AQS is dedicated to quilting excellence. AQS promotes the triumphs of today's quilter, while remaining dedicated to the quilting tradition. We believe in the promotion of this art and craft through AQS Publishing and AQS QuiltWeek®.

CONTENT EDITOR: CAITLIN RIDINGS
GRAPHIC DESIGN: CHRIS GILBERT/ELAINE WILSON
COVER DESIGN: ELAINE WILSON
HOW-TO PHOTOGRAPHY: LARA BUCCELLA
PROJECT SET-UP PHOTOGRAPHY: GINNY BORGIA
PROJECT PHOTOGRAPHY: CHARLES R. LYNCH
ASSISTANT EDITOR: ADRIANA FITCH
PRODUCTION MANAGER: SARAH BOZONE
DIRECTOR OF PUBLICATIONS: KIMBERLY HOLLAND TETREV

All rights reserved. No part of this book may be reproduced, stored in any retrieval system, or transmitted in any form or by any means, including, but not limited to electronic, mechanical, photocopy, recording, or otherwise without the written consent of the author and the publisher. Patterns may be copied for personal use only, including the right to enter contests. Quilter should seek written permission from the author and pattern designer before entering. Credit must be given to the author, pattern designer, and publisher on the quilt label and contest entry form. While every effort has been made to ensure the contents of this publication are accurate and correct, no warranty is provided, nor are results guaranteed. AQS and the author assume no control of individual skill, materials, or tools.

Additional copies of this book may be ordered from the American Quilter's Society, PO Box 3290, Paducah, KY 42002-3290, or online at www.ShopAQS.com.

Attention Photocopying Service: Please note the following—Publisher and author give permission to print pages 82–94.

Text and design © 2016, Lara Buccella
Artwork © 2016, American Quilter's Society

www.AmericanQuilter.com

Library of Congress Cataloging-in-Publication Data

Names: Buccella, Lara, author.Title: Crafted appliquâe : new possibilities / by Lara Buccella.Description: Paducah, KY : American Quilter's Society, [2016]Identifiers: LCCN 2016009045 (print) | LCCN 2016009652 (ebook) | ISBN 9781604603989 (pbk.) | ISBN 9781604603231 (e-book)Subjects: LCSH: Appliquâe--Patterns. | Machine appliquâe--Patterns.Classification: LCC TT779 .B768 2016 (print) | LCC TT779 (ebook) | DDC 746.44/5--dc23LC record available at http://lccn.loc.gov/2016009045